ffer

rofessional development and hands-on resource needs of ource practitioners and gives them products to do their roven ideas and solutions from experts in HR devel- opment and HR management, and we offer effective and customizable tools to improve workplace performance. From novice to seasoned professional, Pfeiffer is the source you can trust to make yourself and your organization more successful.

Essential Knowledge Pfeiffer produces insightful, practical, and comprehensive materials on topics that matter the most to training and HR professionals. Our Essential Knowledge resources translate the expertise of seasoned professionals into practical, how-to guidance on critical workplace issues and problems. These resources are supported by case studies, worksheets, and job aids and are frequently supplemented with CD-ROMs, websites, and other means of making the content easier to read, understand, and use.

Essential Tools Pfeiffer's Essential Tools resources save time and expense by offering proven, ready-to-use materials—including exercises, activities, games, instruments, and assessments—for use during a training or team-learning event. These resources are frequently offered in looseleaf or CD-ROM format to facilitate copying and customization of the material.

Pfeiffer also recognizes the remarkable power of new technologies in expanding the reach and effectiveness of training. While e-hype has often created whizbang solutions in search of a problem, we are dedicated to bringing convenience and enhancements to proven training solutions. All our e-tools comply with rigorous functionality standards. The most appropriate technology wrapped around essential content yields the perfect solution for today's on-the-go trainers and human resource professionals.

Pfeiffer
www.pfeiffer.com

Essential resources for trainin ... *ls*

Practicing Organization Development

**The Change Agent Series
for Groups and Organizations**

MISSION STATEMENT

The books in this series are intended to be cutting-edge, state-of-the-art, innovative approaches to organization change and development. They are written for and by practitioners interested in new approaches to facilitating effective organization change. They are geared to providing both theory and advice on practical applications.

SERIES EDITORS

**William J. Rothwell
Roland Sullivan
Kristine Quade**

EDITORIAL BOARD

**David Bradford
W. Warner Burke
Edith Whitfield Seashore
Robert Tannenbaum
Christopher G. Worley
Shaolin Zhang**

Other Practicing Organization Development Titles

Organization Development at Work

Conversations on the Values, Applications, and Future of OD

Margaret Wheatley   Robert Tannenbaum

Paula Yardley Griffin   Kristine Quade

Organization Development Network

Pfeiffer

A Wiley Imprint

www.pfeiffer.com

Practicing Organization Development

Published by Pfeiffer
An Imprint of Wiley
989 Market Street, San Francisco, CA94103-1741   www.pfeiffer.com

For additional copies/bulk purchases of this book in the U.S. please contact 800-274-4434.

Pfeiffer books and products are available through most bookstores. To contact Pfeiffer directly call our Customer Care Department within the U.S. at 800-274-4434, outside the U.S. at 317-572-3985 or fax 317-572-4002 or www.pfeiffer.com.

Pfeiffer also publishes its books in a variety of electronic formats. Some content that appears in print may not be available in electronic books.

ISBN: 0-7879-6963-X

Library of Congress Cataloging-in-Publication Data

Organization development at work: conversations on the values, applications, and future of OD / Margaret Wheatley .. et al.].
    p. cm.—(The practicing organization development series)
Includes bibliographical references and index.
  ISBN 0-7879-6963-X (alk. paper)
  1. Organizational change. I. Wheatley, Margaret J. II. Series.
  HD58.8.O72835 2003
  658.4′06—dc21
2003006231

Acquiring Editor: Matthew Davis
Director of Development: Kathleen Dolan Davies
Developmental Editor: Susan Rachmeler
Editor: Rebecca Taff

Senior Production Editor: Dawn Kilgore
Manufacturing Supervisor: Bill Matherly
Interior and Cover Design: Bruce Lundquist
Illustrations: Richard Sheppard

Printed in the United States of America

Printing   10   9   8   7   6   5   4   3   2   1

Contents

Dedication
and Reflections

WE WISH TO DEDICATE THIS BOOK to Robert Tannenbaum and the leadership that he provided during his life. At the beginning of this project, Bob and Meg Wheatley scheduled a conversation near Bob's home in California. The night before Meg was to arrive, Bob sat down with us to share some thoughts that were important to him. He wanted these thoughts to convey not only who he was but to include what had created his foundation as a practitioner. We have included some of his points throughout the book. What remains in this dedication is the essence of Bob, which lives deep in our roots. His friend Peter Koestenbaum wrote at his death:

We grieve profoundly for the limits set to life.

We resolve to be worthy of the living gifts of friends and love.

We resolve never to let go of the message and the Commandment, from the Universe itself, that what matters ultimately is to care and to choose to be caring persons.

We resolve to participate more intensely than ever in the Creation of an ethical world, no matter how futile it may seem, for every detail every day is indeed significant.

And out of these resolves grows a new generosity of sprit.

In the Universe nothing is lost. The Universe remembers—be it about atoms or galaxies or noble persons.

Humbled, recalling the eternity of true values, let us commit ourselves to take one more step to earn the golden right to exist.

Then Bob Tannenbaum will have been heard!

July 18, 2001

It's getting near the end (smile), and there are a lot of things I've cared about that I haven't written. I haven't been a prolific writer. Just snippets. I want to talk about the things I care about. What I'd like to do is share with you what I see as the most fundamental underpinnings of OD—the basic notions. Then I realized that there was a lot of hubris in that—that's my view, and there are certainly lots of other views. But that's what I'm going to present—my particular view. So since this is my view, I would like first to introduce myself to those in the profession who don't know me very well or don't know me at all. I think that what I say I believe about the profession will be enhanced by your knowing where I'm coming from.

After my first two years at my local community college, I transferred to the University of Chicago and did the balance of my academic work there. I took liberal arts for the first two years and then mostly business courses. I got my master's in accounting. That was my first specialized field. When I completed my master's degree in 1937, I was fortunate enough to be invited to Oklahoma A&M, now Oklahoma State College, and spent two years there teaching accounting.

In 1939, I decided to go back to Chicago for my doctorate. I began to major in personnel management and industrial relations. That was my first move toward people, a key move on my part. In the early stages of my doctorate, the war was becoming quite hot. I went into the Navy in 1942 for three years. I was on a destroyer in the South and Central Pacific. Word got out that I was a teacher. The Navy started a school called Coconut College on Aore Island in the South Pacific, getting people together from different specializations. Beginning while I was still on a destroyer, and later at Coconut College, I developed a team method of plotting radar data. I designed the work flow so there wasn't time lost as four people worked together. It became accepted as the standard for all destroyers in the Pacific Fleet. I received a commendation from Comdespac for this great contribution to the war effort (smile).

After the war, I came back to the University of Chicago to continue my doctorate. I did some teaching in production management, advanced economic theory, and a little in personnel management. I worked on my dissertation that I later titled *Rational Synthesis of the Manager Complex*. The first part was about the function of managers and the second was about the roots of authority.

In 1948, as I was completing my dissertation, I received an offer to come to UCLA to do work in personnel management and industrial relations. Our recently established Human Relations Research Group (HFFC received a three-year grant from the Office of Navel Research to do research on leadership function). One of the clearly important things was that, for the first time in my career, I was seriously involved in the behavioral sciences. Our student assistants were from clinical psychology, social anthropology, etc. Not long after we received our grant, we were able to leave the personnel management faculty group and started a new major called Behavioral Science for Management. That preceded OD.

Another impactful event occurred in 1951 when I was asked to be a part of the planning committee for the Western Training Laboratory we later called the West Coast Bethel. In that planning committee, we had a number of people who had led groups or been in them and myself and one or two others who did not know what this was all about. The purpose was to get people from various fields who were working on various aspects of human behavior. This planning committee was interdisciplinary. One woman was a professor of dance; she used body movement for personal growth. Another woman was from the psychology department, another from public health. Another key thing, looking back, was that we were all relatively young—late twenties to early forties. We were almost all university-based, mostly from California.

Things that are unplanned often lead to unexpected positive outcomes. I think that that opening of the door, being given the opportunity to move into what we later called sensitivity training, made a huge difference in my life. We professionals were mostly relatively younger men and women. We didn't have to compete with elders who had been in the field successfully for many decades.

It was wide open. We were free to experiment and feel our own way. Our incomes came from our university salaries and our external work was for fees. We weren't motivated by money. The thing that excited us was developing a new field.

Those who were attracted were attracted because of the implicit values and the challenges of this new breakthrough process.

Each laboratory program had a daily general session where members of the separate learning groups came together. Presentations were made by one or more staff members. Joe Luft and Harry Ingram got together for one lab—they got excited about something they'd developed together and called it the Johari Window. Professionally this was very exciting, and for most of us this opportunity to freely incorporate it was the best part of our professional lives. The sharing was unbelievable.

After the first year, a couple of colleagues and I established a new campus course with undergrads and a few graduate students. It was essentially a sensitivity group, but (smile) of course we couldn't call it that so we chose the name "Leadership, Principles, and Practice." That was about 1954. We were real threats to the engineers, economists, mathematicians, and so on, who populated the business schools faculty at that point, and they had a tough time dealing with what we were doing. We were referred to as "the happiness boys." For them, that was the best way they could put us down.

Toward the end of the 1950s, a number of us began to become aware that there was a special problem raided by sensitivity training. You would take people out of their organizations, have them go through the sensitivity training, and then go back to their jobs where there was no one who had shared the same experiences with them. That experience wasn't easily transferable within one's organization. This awareness was key and it gradually led to the development of OD.

There was also another factor that led to the founding of the OD Network. Lee Bradford, the head of National Training Laboratories, realized that there were a number of people in personnel management who had had useful experiences at Bethel or UCLA and he decided it would make sense to get them together. Each individual was trying to find some way of transferring his or her experience of a T-group into the organizational setting. Lee offered a space at Bethel—this was in 1961 or 1962—for these people to come together and talk things over and to share. Which they did. They decided to start a national organization called The Industrial Network. The first meeting was in Estes Park in Colorado—it was designed not for academics, but for practitioners in the field. Fortunately for me, they invited me, Dick Beckhard, Herb Shepard, and fifteen to twenty other people who were working in organizations. Then two or three years later, when Tony Petrella became head of the organization, the name was changed to the OD Network.

While this was happening I had another professionally defining experience. At TRW Systems Group (in Redondo Beach, CA) there was an internal, very creative person named Shel Davis. If you think I'm passionate, you should have seen his passion! While he had been at Harvard, he had heard of this young person teaching at MIT—Herb Shepard—so he went over and took some courses from him. They were impressed with each other, became close friends and mutually respected professional colleagues. Later, Shel began to bring others of us to work with him building a consulting group of around ten externals and ten internals. Over the next ten years or so under Shel's leadership, many innovations in program design and process were creatively experimented with, for example, using sensitivity training for managers to introduce them to new values and a new way of learning about themselves. If today I said to some "here and now" managers that this is what Shel did back then, they'd be scared! After the small group experience, Shel would say, "If there is something you'd like to think about for your own organization unit, let us know and we'll try to be of help to you." He got lots of responses. That's a key lesson—start making progress where there's a readiness.

Now I'm shifting from personal to professional.

A central notion to systems theory is the matter of relationships. You know that story about the butterfly in Africa flapping its wings and starting a major windstorm here. In 1978, James Miller published a book on living systems, just over 1,000 pages. It is a magnum opus and so complex. I have tried to read it many times. What I got out of it has just blown my mind. But it told me that systems notions were either implicitly or explicitly in the air as early as the 1940s.

Miller identified a number of characteristics of all systems: the molecule, the cell, the organism, the group, the organization, and the supranation. In each chapter, dealing at each of these levels, he used the key characteristics of all systems and showed how each characteristic plays itself out at each of these levels. I have a deep belief without any proof that this uniformity that Miller sees starting with the atom goes on through the universe. Awesome is the best word I have been able to find to capture the simplicity, the relative similarity in structure and function, from the cell to the universe. It's beautiful and awesome.

Deep change of any system is not easy to facilitate. For any system to go through change is terribly painful. I have a feeling that we are still pretty primitive people. To face the unknown, to have comfortable tolerance for ambiguity is hard. I don't believe that many people have that tolerance.

Another aspect besides the similarity of systems and basic characteristics at all levels is the thrust toward wholeness, the thrust away from fragmentation. I hope that however we work, we recognize the dissonant parts of those systems and direct our energies toward working for wholeness. What guides us in working toward wholeness are our values. For me, and this is a strong bias, the value is the centrality of the individual. As I was sorting through my things, I ran into something. In the front of the national OD membership roster, there is two-thirds of a page on our values: collaboration, cooperation, knowledge of self, social responsibility, social justice—those go all the way from the individual up to society. These are what I'd call humanistic values, which I have been guided by for the past years. But there are a few that are missing.

Authenticity as a goal is a value. Non-authenticity is not wholeness. Until one is authentic, one is not whole. Another is trust and trust building, which in the international scene today is so central to solving the problems and is not strong enough for those problems to be solved.

Now the next thing I'd like to talk about is change. What do we mean by change? Change for what? Most of our writings are written with the implicit notion that the change we are seeking is good. But not all change is good. Picture Hitler with some OD consultants . . . this becomes a value question.

Change is constantly mentioned. But what about stability? There isn't too much written about this either. Rarely do we go into an organization and suggest a complete overhaul of everything. I have no proof—just an intuitive sense—that very often you make the most progress by focusing on change in part of a system and maintaining stability in the balance of the system. If everything changes, people can't deal with it all. Stability is a concept that we haven't given enough attention to. We ought to be looking at them together and trying to understand them in that context.

So, what about techniques and methods? I have some concern about the word "competencies." I would like to capture a different meaning. People have to be good listeners and communicators, for example; those are competencies. But there is something more important there, in the area of wholeness. The art of the concept is when all of these are meaningfully integrated within the person. So often, especially in working with students and interns, one of the first things people want to know is, "How to do this?" Their anxiety in going out and practicing; this is, "What do I do?" So they want to reach into their bag of tricks, rather than really being at one with the flow of what's happening in the organization, in one's self, and what's relevant to that flow.

I am convinced that to really make change involves going through a lot of pain and fear and being able to move on. This is not something that happens by the books. In psychotherapy, there's not a question that in a lot of areas, each of us has accomplished about as much as we can do in personal growth. I doubt that we change very much in terms of the deeper aspects of our being.

My comments about systems are ones that I would also make about process and flow. If you're going to flow with the river, there is a highly intuitive demand being placed on you. You have to have a lot of tolerance for ambiguity, and you also have to be relevant to what's happening. I am convinced that if a person does not have a reasonably good knowledge of him- or herself, then our not knowing becomes our greatest enemy. Therefore, intuition and comfort with not knowing are what help us to deal with chaos.

I believe that the self is a laboratory for learning. I am a system, just like this department, like this organization, and I am constantly having to deal with fractionalization within me. I can make attempts to wall off, hide, or cover myself in maskmanship. But if I can be aware of what's going on in me and how to deal with that, I know that this personal work will present analogies to the client system where I am working. Essentially the same things are happening at several levels. Working at the self level in an ongoing basis is a wonderful way to get a better understanding of the other systems we are encountering.

This now leads full circle to conditional and unconditional love as the reason for getting to know oneself better. Until we are able to love ourselves, and not for a reward for doing it, we cannot love someone else unconditionally. Since a lot of our work is tied up in relationships, if we are unable to do it within ourselves, we aren't able to do it with others.

So for me there is a giant interconnectedness between the system, the values that guide us, our understanding of change, and our knowledge of the process of change. The anchor in our work is that we do it with our person. Pretty simple and pretty complex. That is why my work in this field has me so awe-struck. It is just awesome!

Post Script: Bob finished his final edit of this reflection within days of his death on March 14, 2003. He wanted to make sure he had completed his contribution to this book as his "final gift" to the field of OD.

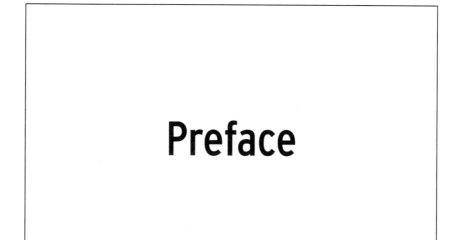

Preface

THIS BOOK IS A CHILD OF THE INTERNET, an example of the ways technology unites communities and enables exploration of ideas. The idea for "a book based on a conversation" developed when Roland Sullivan, one of the editors of the Practicing OD Series, observed that the sharing on the listserv of the Organization Development Network reflected some of the best thinking around. After Roland recruited a project team, we envisioned inviting hundreds of OD practitioners into a wide-ranging conversation—discussing topics from groundbreaking new concepts to practical and grounded application tips regarding both emerging and well-used models.

The OD Network, with its experience with conducting online conferences through the MetaNetwork, suggested we try that vehicle for involving others. It was just the right venue for holding a conversation that might last for many weeks, for providing information about the conversation and its purpose, and for managing some of the administrative tasks required in publishing that would have become unwieldy if done with standard methods. Just obtaining permission to use the words of more than one hundred contributors could have overwhelmed the most dedicated support staff.

The project engaged our imaginations from the beginning. It was an opportunity to showcase the brains, experience, breadth, talent, and generosity of a group of people who have made the field of organization development an exciting place to be. From the lively and challenging initial conversation between Meg Wheatley and Bob Tannenbaum, to the months-long conversation among some of the most extraordinary professionals in any field, one thing that has differentiated this conversation is the very thing that draws many of us to the field of OD—variety.

The conversation was actually launched in person, as Meg Wheatley and Bob Tannenbaum sat in easy chairs near Bob's Carmel, California, home, considering the field from all angles and exploring their differing perspectives. Bob and Meg brought two very different and important perspectives to the foundation of the conversation. Bob was a member of the field before it was a field. He understood its roots, its underlying values, the inner core that keeps it strong in a changing world. He was among the people who can claim to have founded a field of work. Meg is one of the challenging thinkers of our day, a person whose presence in a room enables discussions of such lofty ideas as applying the principles of science to organizations, and reconsidering the concept of globalization. She has inspired many to think more broadly, more purposefully, about our relationship with our world.

When Meg and Bob kicked off the conversation, they posed a number of questions they thought might generate interest (reflected in the Freeze Frames at the beginning of each chapter). They were concerned that people might not have enough to talk about. They needn't have worried. The conversation took off quickly as OD professionals long accustomed to using the Internet to accomplish their work jumped in to share stories, ask questions, provide answers, challenge, and enlighten.

Participants responded with enthusiasm, telling the stories of how they came to find the field, their purpose in it, and the focus of their service. For some, OD was an accidental discovery on the way to where they thought they were headed. For others, OD was a fit for their values or the answer to questions they had been asking. For a few, but only a few, OD was the original destination. You will find those stories distributed throughout the book.

Participants were most generous in sharing the theory bases, ideas, models, and tools they use in their work—not the theory as written, but the theory as used and adapted in the field. We found the conversation to be in many ways like having a long talk with our favorite mentors, people who tell us what really works.

When the conversation was closed online, Paula Griffin and Kristine Quade began the process of editing all those conversations. Again, the Internet was the venue of choice as chapters sailed back and forth between Minnesota (Kristine), Pennsylvania (Paula), and California (Susan Rachmeler, developmental editor for the Practicing OD Series).

All this sharing has produced a book that we believe most OD practitioners will find thought-provoking and useful and that new practitioners will find essential. It will be a place to turn to hear experienced consultants and senior practitioners discuss such topics as:

- Do we serve the client or something else?
- Are we based in humanistic values or business values?
- How are we distinguished from related fields?
- What are the principles and values people who've worked in the field for years actually base their practice on?
- How do the models we use every day differ from the models we were taught?
- What are the differences international practitioners have found as they adapt OD to other cultures?
- Is OD dying? If not, what will it look like in the future?
- And so much more.

How This Book Is Organized

Chapter 1, Questions of Identity, invites participants to consider the foundations of their OD practice. What are the definitions and boundaries of the OD field? What drew them to the field? What energizes their work? Whom do we serve? The answers to all these questions uncover some of the clear divisions in the field and may illustrate why identity questions continue to recur.

Chapter 2, Principles in Action, tackles the critical questions around the principles and values on which our field, and our individual practices, are based. In a field that professes to be based on values, there can be no more important discussion. Yet the principles and values we espouse differ from person to person, and often from what we act on as well.

Chapter 3, Models and Methods, asks practitioners to share the foundational theories of their practices and the models that have made a difference for them and their clients over the years. Conversation participants described many models that have been effective in organizations and the changes they had made to those models in their practices. Few models are applied in their "vanilla" form; we like to tinker. The tinkerings described here range from simple adjustments to full rewrites based on the needs of specific clients and sectors.

Chapter 4, Global Practice of OD, looks at the significant learning by experienced practitioners as they extend their practices beyond the western perspectives of OD. This chapter provides an examination of the variables and awareness of the complexity of a global OD practice.

Chapter 5, The Future, considers the wishes, dreams, and predictions of participants for the future of this field we call our profession. It becomes clear that we are at a juncture of "then and now" as a variety of points of view provoke our thinking about what we are as a practice field and where we are going.

Paula Griffin and Kristine Quade served as moderators of the conversation and as occasional contributors, but primarily as editors sifting volumes of marvelous contributions down to an amount manageable for a book. It was exceedingly difficult to eliminate some of the wonderful thoughts that occurred in the online conversation in order to meet the necessary length restrictions of publication. And we know this: Like the river, the conversation continues. We have dipped our bucket at this moment to drink of its knowledge, and will do so again at other times in other ways. The book is a snapshot, if you will, of a point in the ongoing conversation about our field.

To facilitate the continuing conversation, we have offered a list of questions at the beginning and end of each chapter. These "Freeze Frames" include questions that began this conversation and questions that arose because of it. We hope readers will take a few moments to consider these questions for themselves, and perhaps to join with others to consider them in groups. The exercise will assist them in clarifying their own thoughts on the topics and in integrating new concepts, principles, and theories into their own practices.

Acknowledgments

IT'S NOT EASY to single out for thanks a few people among the hundreds who participated in this project. The generosity we have experienced in the course of this project has been an inspiration. So it is with profound gratitude that we acknowledge first the contributors who offered so generously their insights and ideas. There are a few people, however, without whom this quite simply would not have happened.

Roland Sullivan's vision and energy conceived the project. Roland is truly a catalyst.

Bob Tannenbaum and Meg Wheatley launched the conversation in style. Bob was willing to give this project precious time and energy at a time when he was limiting his professional obligations to focus on family and friends, bringing closure to a long and productive career. Bob spent many hours in articulating a summary of his life and values, which provided the launching of the conversation. Meg flew from a meeting in Europe to spend a weekend with Bob and the other authors. She fit this work into a strenuous speaking schedule somehow, and we are so glad she did.

Marti Kaplan captured the audio of the conversation at the same time the video was capturing Bob and Meg. She then spent long hours making sure the content was fully captured. Marti's gentle and supportive work helped us begin to shape the project.

Matt Minahan sponsored the conversation on the MetaNetwork and served as trainer and technical guru for those who had trouble navigating the intricacies of modern web architecture. From designing the conference site to helping people with forgotten passwords, Matt is a model of servant leadership.

Doug Griffin, Paula's husband, used his creativity and experience to suggest technologies and designs for the conversation and for the book. When we were stumped, he was not.

Amy Herman deployed the resources of the OD Network to help this conversation happen, and without the assistance of her and her staff it would never have come to pass.

Mirlande Parker and Jaqueline Meyers supported us with additional administrative tasks that are necessarily part of an innovative project like this. We are so grateful.

Susan Rachmeler is the kind of editor who gently moves a work toward the best it can be. Her questions, suggestions, and patience are endlessly helpful.

In addition, Kristine wishes to thank her husband, Kent Hann, for reading over her shoulder, cheering from the side, and all the neck massages. A big thank you goes to Paula Griffin and her professionalism. She is an editor of extraordinary competence and never missed a deadline. You were a joy to collaborate with! Aw shucks, says Paula, and notes that Kristine Quade managed to navigate the roles of author, editor, and series honcho very, very gracefully.

Organization Development at Work

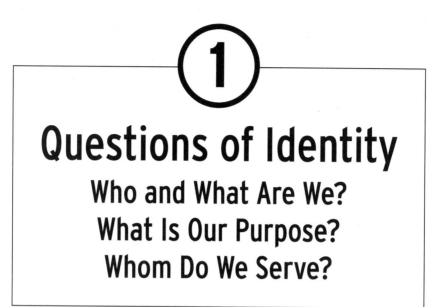

Questions of Identity
Who and What Are We?
What Is Our Purpose?
Whom Do We Serve?

• FREEZE FRAME

Before and after each chapter in this book, we will include questions for your personal consideration or group discussion. Some of these questions arose from the initial conversation between Bob Tannenbaum and Meg Wheatley, while others have been suggested by the online conversation among more than one hundred practitioners. The questions will help you to connect this material to your own beliefs, experience, and practice and to integrate new ideas.

In this chapter we consider the questions of identity: our purpose and whom we serve. Take a few minutes to consider your thoughts on the questions below before beginning this chapter.

1. For me, what are the boundaries of the field of OD? What fields is OD related to, and how? Is it important that those boundaries be clear? Why or why not?

2. What was the purpose, if any, that brought me into the field of OD? How does that purpose relate to the work I take on?

3. As I consider my purpose and work in the field, whom do I serve? Do I consider the focus of my service to be a single client, the organization, the employees, a higher power, myself, society as a whole, or something else?

•   •   •

Identity

We begin, as we do in each of the sections of this conversation, with the discussion between Meg Wheatley and Bob Tannenbaum.

Meg Wheatley

What I'm interested in, Bob, is the continuity that you've seen in all these years. As you look out now and into the future, what do you see that feels like it's continuous, and what do you see that might signify a radical break? That's what intrigues me.

Bob Tannenbaum

I don't think that in a major way we're facing a paradigm shift. Consider systems theory. People in our field, and related fields, began talking in systems terms going back before the 1920s. Eric Trist and Fred Emery at the Tavistock Institute were using systems approaches for a long time. I have a quote from Trist that actually uses the phrase self-organizing.

Then I think of sensitivity training, which started at Bethel in 1947. As a trainer, you walk into the group with no agenda, no traditional leadership, and things are wide open. More recently, one of the trends of the field has been to move toward large group interventions, where one of the phrases used is "getting everyone into the room." But what happens again, what takes place, is what happens in a T-group. In a sense, some of the best things we've done in the past fifty years have been *systems oriented*, a tremendous awareness of relationships, interconnections, of minimizing to the extent possible the expression of control and authority. There are so many examples of that both in writings and in action from the field.

For me, through the years, the field of OD has been primarily defined by, and gained its identity through, several basic qualities:

- It has increasingly focused on human systems at all levels, from the individual to the inter-organizational;

- Its basic concern has been with systems change; and

- Its practitioners have been guided by humanistic values.

Organization development practitioners have primarily been specialists in facilitating change processes—helping client systems to move in directions desired by that system—rather than activists using the client system as a vehicle for the attainment of their own goals.

Nevertheless, increasingly these qualities do not demark the field. There are many others who are concerned with systems, change, values, and processes—other consultants, diplomats, arbitrators, conciliators, counselors and therapists, managers, teachers, parents. All of these specialists, and more, share overlapping theories, concepts, and methods (although they may be designated by differing language).

I have predicted, and continue to predict, that a new field is emerging that will break down present boundaries and will coalesce at least many of these present specialties under one change-developing body of theories, concepts, and methods. Groups might be differentiated by the focuses of the entities, such as business organizations, international political relations, classroom, home, and so on. My preference for a designation of this emerging umbrella field is Human Systems Development.

Meg Wheatley

It's true. We see that the issue of identity of the field is so important; it guides who joins the field and what they believe about their own purpose. It is the source of organization and, as such, a source of energy. So it matters very much. Identity applies to everything, whether it's at the individual level or the nation state—a relationship, a team, or a field of work. We need to be together asking: What are we trying to be? What's possible now? How can the world be different because of us?

So as we consider our identity and purpose, we must consider the world. We must ask ourselves: What will the world need from us and our field in the future, and how can that help us define ourselves? I believe the world is in a dire situation now. This is not the time to tinker with our field. It is time to ask ourselves, "What is going on—the big picture?" The skills and processes of OD are needed during this time, needed as they have never been needed. Who do we need to be, with what we know, during this time of planetary crisis? What is our purpose? What do we want to give voice to?

Bob Marshak

I believe we as a profession are losing our roots and purpose and, therefore, our identity. We don't have an agenda anymore, nor do we have practitioners who can think psychologically. Many new practitioners are hanging on to something they don't understand. Here is some of what I believe OD is and is not:

OD is value-based. Our roots come from human psychology: Maslow, McGregor, Argyris, and the notion of psychology of potential, growth, and development. We were values-based early on. The OD value is not about change but about change that makes people better—humanistic values.

For example, we might ask workers to have input into a solution because we had the notion that they would be more committed to plan. However, the "value" reason would be "more input gives better results." If we involve workers in order to have them become committed to our plan, we are manipulating. We would be seeking input only for the sake of buy-in, an invitation to participate without the belief of the competency or ability of others. Another principle is a belief that all input is valid, that it provides a diversity of viewpoints, and therefore the results will be better because of the input process.

Today, we have practitioners using interventions without understanding the values they are based on. We do not have practitioners who are looking for new theory. We have moved from a field that was at the margin to one that is in the mainstream. Our interventions are different from the early ones. They are marketplace-driven. We have co-opted our ability to confront the organization so that we can remain marketable.

OD is about people. If people are the variable, then the practitioner is doing OD. If the variable is about a process, a strategy, or an intervention, then the practitioner is not doing OD. This is not to say it is not honorable or without contribution. But OD is values-based.

Some people think of OD as facilitation of a meeting or a big event. No. The OD practitioner has to know a lot at many levels, which includes how the business operates as well as how individuals operate. The primary tool for our work is the use of self, which includes use of character and personage, a developed mind, strong theory foundation, and the ability to stretch into different bodies of knowledge.

In the past we believed that if the people side were right, the business side would go right. Now, practitioners often don't understand the people side, and the shift is to try to understand the business side. Sadly enough, there is not much theory for integrating the two. In one sense, OD was about liberating tight constraints.

Now organizations are not bureaucratic, but the struggle is among different elements, such as financial and economic drivers, bottom line, ROI, and shareholder equity, which are a new form of tight constraints.

I believe we are afraid to own the values of OD because we fear we will not get work. We are disingenuous and colluding when we enter into a situation out of alignment with our values.

OD respects its founders. The early founders were people who believed in self-actualization, humanistic and social psychology, social justice, democratic process, equity, and empowerment values of OD. They were the early connectors in beliefs, theory, and practice. They were the ones who embodied the values that are so core to OD. The founders of OD had Ph.D.s in social psychology. They had to know group dynamics very, very well in order to be a T-group facilitator or a group facilitator. Now, it seems that interventions are just orchestrated programs. The skill level of working with group dynamics is missing. The founders can help us with the language of why we do what we do. So, let's study our roots.

Chris Worley

I happen to believe that OD is alive and well. But if you listen to those who believe that OD is dead or dependent on the reputations of well-known practitioners, you can see how it got into this situation. The field's definitions are fuzzy, its most successful interventions have become institutionalized, and it's too easy to call yourself an OD practitioner.

The problem begins with the definitions and boundaries of organization development. Although there are more than a dozen definitions of OD, most suggest that it concerns system-wide planned change, uses behavioral science interventions, targets human and social processes of organizations (specifically the belief systems of individuals, work groups, or culture), and intends to build the capacity to adapt and renew organizations. Moreover, there is considerable overlap in the activities and interventions listed within most OD textbooks.

Almost every OD intervention is claimed by at least one other discipline. Reward system and performance management interventions are considered part of human resource management; leadership and strategic change methodologies are shared with the strategy and business policy discipline; and reengineering is practiced by industrial engineers and information technologists.

Where do these other fields end and OD begin, or vice versa? Where do emerging issues, such as environmental or sustainability auditing, creating an internal information system knowledge base, or managing cross-cultural organizations belong? These fuzzy boundaries make it difficult to determine what OD is and what it is not.

Another reason for OD's weak reputation is that it may be a victim of its own success. Many of the techniques and interventions invented and practiced by OD professionals have become "mainstream." Team building is as prevalent in organizations as budget planning. Organization surveys, feedback, and problem-solving meetings are considered a normal part of organization life. The issues and interventions that were once closely identified with organization development are now part of traditional business practice.

Finally, OD has shot itself in the foot by coddling a variety of untrained and inexperienced people. In its attempt to be inclusive, people who do not have the background, education, or experience to support an organization through complex change can call themselves OD practitioners. The most misunderstood qualification of being an OD practitioner is the most fundamental: the role of personal growth and self-development.

Too many people enter the field of OD because its roots are in the counterdependent tradition of overthrowing oppression. Some people who call themselves practitioners are doing the work to overthrow a generalized belief that all management regimes are authoritarian . . . and they are unaware of that motivation. When people become "OD practitioners" because they think organizations "should" be changed, because they were treated unfairly in an earlier context, or because all managers are bad, and there is no awareness of these motivations, OD becomes a "cause."

Personal growth work is central to the practice of OD because it helps to answer the question, "Whose needs are you working?" Unfortunately, too many practitioners are working their own needs, are unaware of those needs, and are unconsciously intervening in organizations to alter power and authority distributions when that may or may not be appropriate. These self-proclaimed OD practitioners unconsciously promote their view of "right" without concern for the organization's current state, strategy, or values, and that hurts the field's reputation.

Building on Bob Marshak's earlier comments, I think an important first step is to better define OD. To my mind, for an activity to be labeled OD it must:

- Involve change in some system;

- Intend to improve the effectiveness of that system; and

- Build capacity in the system to manage itself in the future.

If an effort labeled OD does not involve change, then I think there's too much overlap between OD and other disciplines like human resource management or organization behavior. If it is not intended to improve the effectiveness of the system, then I think accusations of irrelevance may be justified. And perhaps most importantly, I think that learning must be involved. Unless the effort builds capacity in the client system, then there's little chance of distinguishing OD from change management.

A second important step in creating an identity for OD is getting clearer about the qualifications. While I'm against certification, I do think the market needs to be educated about its consumption of consultants. To be an OD practitioner, people need to have demonstrated self-knowledge, a broad understanding of theory and practice, and supervised experience.

Finally, I believe the field needs a more coordinated effort to articulate the "values" it thinks are so important. There are at least three different efforts underway by the OD Network, the OD Institute, and the Ethics Clearinghouse. If each one competes with the other to come up with the "right" or "best" list, the field will become increasingly fragmented.

Organization development is a powerful technology that can help organizations manage change, achieve objectives, and implement strategies. While many have pronounced OD dead or dying, these prognostications have been occurring for twenty years. OD, like other behavioral science disciplines, is going through its growing pains, and there is every reason to believe that it will thrive and survive into the future.

Glenda Eoyang

I agree with Dr. Tannenbaum when he says that a new field is emerging. He says this field "will coalesce at least many of these present specialties under one change-developing body of theories, concepts, and models."

As I see it, if we don't find a way to coalesce, the energy and focus of the field will continue to dissipate. Practitioners will find it even more difficult to describe our work to their clients. Scholars will focus on more and more subtle differences within the field while they miss the major transformations beyond it. Researchers will continue to wrestle with methods and findings that are either overly simplistic or not generalizable. Standards of practice will continue to weaken as more and more people do the work with less and less understanding.

We can avoid this slide into entropy and disorder, but we need a new way to conceptualize our work so that we can incorporate the rich learnings of the past and build a framework to carry our discoveries and applications into the future.

William Gellermann

I too would like to emphasize the point made by Bob Tannenbaum when he said, "My preference for a designation of this emerging umbrella field is Human Systems Development." Human Systems Development (HSD) is the field with which I identify. If we collectively were to identify with that field, many of us could still focus on businesses and corporations, while others focus on the whole range of other systems (for example, individuals, team building, communities, nations, or transnational networks) and some of us focus on the global governance system.

D. Kirk Hamilton

As Chris Worley and others have noted, the field of OD overlaps with the edges of a good many other fields. But from some of those fields there are important principles that we in OD should consider. Take physical space. As an architect entering the OD field, I'm surprised by the lack of material on the physical environment. Architects frequently are involved in the planned change of organizations at the request of their clients. They rarely have a foundation of organization theory to assist or guide them. Architects live on the technical side of the socio-technical model.

But OD practitioners seem not to consider the physical environment. Most definitions of the environment in OD books talk only of the larger external cultural or regulatory environment, or the environment as something with which the organization transacts inputs or outputs. In 1973, Fred Steele wrote a small book in the Addison-Wesley series, *Physical Settings and Organization Development*. He is one of the few to relate the immediate physical environment or setting of the individual, group, or task to OD.

Why is there so little attention to the profound effect of the physical environment on the organization? Is the physical design of architecture or interior design a legitimate OD intervention? If so, OD practitioners should be prepared to consider the efficacy of a physical intervention and the advantage of collaborating with a design professional.

Purpose
Meg Wheatley

I believe we need to look now at the answers to some important questions. We must ask ourselves who we need to be in this profession, at this time, in this world. We must consider our purpose in our work with increased consciousness—or we continue to contribute to what I see as a huge problem. We have decided we can make up our own rules for being on this planet. We don't have to follow life's rules. We're playing God and ignoring the generic rules of the game. We thought we could grow forever. We've decided that we don't have to go through the cycles of life. We have created the mess we're in. But there's an ecology principle that we've forgotten: Nature always has the last word.

Bob Tannenbaum

There is a statement in your writings, Meg, that I very much agree with—the necessity to go through the dark side in major change. Therapists have held that central to how they work all the time. The holding on/letting go/moving on lab that Bob Hanna and I did at Bethel had the same orientation.

There are some really new things—particularly in chaos theory—that strike me. But as I look at it, and I'm open to being convinced otherwise, I see a bigger challenge in the number of people who are reached with an awareness of what's already there in value terms. We have a lot of accumulated wisdom already about these kinds of things.

Meg Wheatley

I agree, Bob. You're right that some things are constant, such as values. We still need to go through the dark side to accomplish major change. As they did in the earliest T-group, facilitators need to be ready for whatever happens in a group.

But some things are so very different. The increasing interconnectedness of everything and everyone means that our actions can have an impact on others unknown. One person can have a strong impact through either fear or love. You mention chaos, Bob. We are surprised with unimaginable events. There is the power of one—the terrorist who changes millions of lives. Most people do not know or want to know the extent to which they are interconnected.

I've been watching failure of the old paradigm. Corporations, major consulting firms, schools, governments, and churches cannot look past the immediate project. Is the system developing greater capacity or unraveling? It is hard to provide a solution to what we helped create. We don't have the means or resources to solve these problems and we don't understand the consequences. We solve one problem and create twenty more.

I believe that, in the war of values, there has been a victory. Market values have won: individualism, competition, speed, and greed. How can we compete through materialism if we don't subscribe to these market values? We believe we wouldn't be seen as progressive or modern.

But there is no future in a system based on individualism, profit at all cost, or growth at all cost. OD has always been a profession of idealists, people for whom service meant more than money, and for whom purpose was more at the heart level. We have to find a way into the middle of the mess. The eyes of the truly hungry people are on us. What are they hungry for? What is not happening that people are longing for?

Turning to one another is an essential gesture. Are we engaged in a profession helping to move toward a web, or are we doing what we are asked to do? We are in a good place to help, to honor values of being truly human. That is our identity and purpose.

Kathleen Dannemiller

The driving force of my personal work in organization development has been to help every voice be heard. How we do that is always different, but for me the method has been to work with microcosms of the organization, get them listening to each other in a way that brings out each person's truth and accepts it as truth, then combine yearnings of everyone into a compelling vision of where we need to be going together, and then to come up with our own answers as to what will get us there. Probably the most important truths for me are encapsulated in that statement: Let every voice be heard and each person's truth be true.

Steve Cady (of Bowling Green University) and I have been doing some research into the commonalities among people who have started whole system technologies (the one I started so many years ago is called Whole-Scale Change, but there are a good number of others). We've learned that there are five "truths" these people agree on. Each of us, and all of us, see the following:

- *Systems.* We simply see, believe, and breathe system.
- *Purpose.* There are no throwaway lines in our lives. In any part of the system we enter, we are always "on purpose."
- *Change Journey.* We all recognize change as a journey, not just a "one-time" fix-it happening.
- *Theory Base.* All of our work is rooted in robust theory.
- *Values.* Everything we do, in every part of our life journey, is based consistently on values.

Jeff McCollum

The purpose that drives my work is helping organizations serve their key stake-holders (customers, employees, and investors) with distinction. The "develop-ment" part of OD is what inspires me—developing people and organizations of distinction.

When we are far enough out into the future to see the 20th Century in full per-spective, I think we will see the industrial organization as an aberration in human development that valued financial assets over human ones, polluted the planet, and created jobs that were spiritual prisons for people in them. I think OD emerged as an antidote to the ills of the industrial model that has subsequently become the model for most organizations (see Mintzberg's "Machine Bureaucracy").

The exciting thing about being in this field now is that we are collectively engaged in helping organizations produce idiosyncratic models/forms in response to the changes in the environment.

And I worry a bit. Years ago I saw a training movie, the name of which I can't remember, but the thesis has stayed with me since. The thesis is that organiza-tions/agencies arise to deal with a societal problem and wind up with a vested interest in the problem. Police have a vested interest in crime. Ministers have a vested interest in sin. Do we have a vested interest in the perpetuation of organi-zational dysfunction?

Chuck Phillips

Like others in this conversation, I am working to balance the really good work of my organization and its products with the best interests of its people, including myself. I see as part of my purpose to be challenging the organization and its lead-ership to always be planning, making decisions, strategizing, and so forth, in the context of their responsibility to the multitude of legitimate stakeholders.

Judith H. Katz

I deeply connect to the purpose that people have expressed here: to make the world a better place. I was fortunate to be a child of the 1960s. For me, OD is deeply rooted in a set of values and principles of change, social justice, equality, and participa-tion. OD has always meant knowing myself and using myself as an instrument for change. One of the lessons I learned early on was to trust my experience and emo-tions as real data, to know what my limits are as well as how my identities (as a white, Jewish, heterosexual woman) and experiences impact my practice. I was drawn to OD because it requires all of me to be fully engaged and to recognize that the change is not only out there but also in me.

After more than twenty-five years as an OD practitioner, I am still optimistic that change is possible—that we can make the world and the organizations in which we work better places, creating workplaces that work for us all. OD is at the forefront of this change. This is the new frontier—the human frontier—to stretch beyond what has been. Being a part of such change fuels my passion, purpose, and being.

Bev Scott

When I started practicing OD in 1973, it seemed to me that OD's purpose was centered on helping to change organizations to be better places for human beings to work, especially the disenfranchised, those at the bottom, and those who were different. This humanistic, value-based approach matched my own values and I was excited to find this field for my career. Such a purpose required providing opportunities for members of organizations to give voice, participate, and become involved in the decision process. It was also clear that in order to really be effective in supporting change in both individuals and in organizations, we as practitioners had to be self-aware and know our own issues and hang-ups first.

Over time as an external and internal OD consultant, I observed and participated in the shift that focused on influencing managers and leaders to be more effective (which would ultimately impact employees) and to meet their organizational goals.

The increased focus on shareholder value in the mid-1980s pushed managers to take the actions, such as downsizing, business process re-engineering, mergers, and acquisitions, that have resulted in increasingly oppressive and disruptive work environments. We saw business consultants use techniques and methodologies from OD and call it change management. We, as a field, became timid and uncertain. Had we lost our values? Was OD out-of-date? Could we help leaders become more effective in accomplishing goals we no longer believed in? Could we influence leaders from our original purpose and value base?

I think that our values base is what distinguishes our field from others that use similar technology. Today, values such as having choice, giving voice, valuing a balanced life, and sustainability are critical to the future of not only our field but also for organizations. These values are the foundation of our purpose and identity.

Steve Cady

Like many others in this field, my purpose is related to values. I value bringing people together from all walks of life—multiple perspectives, conditions, values, beliefs, and attitudes. It is my goal to create communities of diverse people supporting each other in living their dreams and doing the necessary personal work to support their dreams being realized.

When I started working in OD, my goal was to make a lot of money first, and then I would pursue my purpose more fully. A mentor of mine gave me some advice you've probably heard before: "Do what you love, and the money will follow." So I flipped things around and focused on my purpose first. It was at that very moment the wonder of my life journey opened up. I often think of the question, "Did I do that on purpose?" I am reminded of the power of purpose. By staying on purpose, I have found OD and the many opportunities it affords me to richly live—a passionate life—a life of my dreams.

Glenn Allen-Meyer

I entered the field in the mid-1980s. I was tremendously energized by the ways in which people at work seemed to open themselves up during sessions (training programs, T-groups, and so on) and during their participation in change. This, to me, was like a grand flowering of what I thought human potential could be. I was instantly taken by the field and knew I would become part of it in some way. My challenge and purpose was simple: I wanted to be part of helping people find and use their voice and their talent at work.

By the early 1990s, something had changed. "How could it be," I wondered to myself, "that people who seemed so interested in change now seem so cynical?" I started hearing terms like "flavor of the month" being used to describe processes that had filled me and others with such excitement just a few years earlier.

My purpose then split into two streams that guide my work today. The first stream is about identifying the individual, group, organizational, and societal biases that limit people's ability to bring their voices to work—to be fully themselves in a way that adds undreamed of value to their places of work—and have a positive impact on those situations.

The second stream involves studying the basic assumptions of organization development, which, over the years, have become co-opted by organizational change infrastructures that tend to "market" change to people at work in order to gain economies of scale during the change process. People at work today—used to SPAM, telemarketers, and targeted marketing campaigns—recognize hype when they experience it and respond with compliance, at best, and, at worst, with resistance that leads to lateness, turnover, accidents, and other forms of dysfunction.

My light remains strong, however. The feelings I felt when I first started—the sense that I had become part of something tremendously right for people—continues. Inside the cynical response to marketed and hyped change, I still find many, many reasons to work to uncover opportunities for my own voice and for hearing the voices of others.

John Agno

At certain times in life, most people take stock of where they are and where they want to go. Deciding what is important to us during our life's journey, including where we may be stuck, is a good way to begin this mid-course correction. The gift of knowing who we are and what we are meant to do helps us set a forward life direction—both personally and professionally.

Unfortunately, most people begin this life purpose investigation situationally—from where they are in their work (like their OD career), in their relationship with spouse and family, and in consideration of all those competing commitments that drain one's available energy—rather than looking inwardly to unlock their dreams. Working on the intangible, inward, ideal-self stuff (assumptions/beliefs, values, vision, and guiding principles) is what it takes to become aware of one's real identity.

Once you know who you really are, you can begin to articulate what you were meant to do—your "purpose." Then, and only then, is one able to cross the purpose bridge from the intangible to a tangible action plan that can take one to where he or she wants to be. Using this inward to outward process helps bring clarity by:

- Becoming self-aware of the "should roles" we have been playing based on our inherited or traditional purpose—which has resulted in our unconscious default behavior. Just being aware of our traditional roles and purpose allows us to begin to choose the behavior that is representative of who we really are and wish to be.

- Articulating who we really are (rather than who we are expected to be), writing it down, and testing our assumptions brings a tremendous energy focus that can push us along in attunement with our discovered purpose. Without this internal work, we have no "go to" purpose statement that keeps us in alignment.

Those competing commitments of the present continue to diffuse our available energy and pull us in many different directions, making it difficult to move forward.

Robert McCarthy

I came to OD work in the hope of finding a more effective way to facilitate change after a difficult early experience as a troubleshooter for a CEO. I found the problems, but making the needed changes was painful and slow. I thought there just had to be a better way to improve performance.

I notice that what remains of the work is the growth of the individual. Everything else is subject to entropy and dissolution through mergers, new leadership, and so forth. What lasts and what continues to inspire me are innovative projects that become models for others and the growth of leaders at every level.

These individuals are doing the work we used to do. They have acquired the skills and the knowledge of OD methods to lead their organization improvement work without consultants. My conclusion is that OD is a field of work. The profession is "third party," and the job is transferring the knowledge of the tools to the organization.

Paula Griffin

Robert, I like your comment that what remains in our work, after the organizational changes and tides of organizational centralization and decentralization, is the growth of the individual. As a veteran of more than one downsizing, merger, or centralization shift, I've seen months' (or years) worth of work disappear in a whirl of memos neatly filed by project, or client, or year. It can be discouraging if your purpose was to complete the project that was cancelled or improve the organization that disappeared in the merger. When our goal or purpose is to improve the human condition or to help individuals to improve themselves, there is always something to look back on and something to look forward to.

John Adams

Paula's comment makes me think of sustainability, which has been a theme for me. I have long believed we must become more involved in broader perspectives, longer time frames, and more systemic and socially responsible ways of considering our work. It's beginning to happen. In a 1992 survey of what it is important for OD to consider, only 7 percent of the responses expressed any sense of the future being different from the present. In an early 2002 Delphi process on the future competencies that OD people will need (conducted by Saul Eisen), there was a very central presence of the need to pay attention to issues of sustainability and social responsibility in the future.

So as I move into the sage stage of my life (sixty this year—yikes!), I am finding that my purpose is very focused on bringing awareness to individual and collective thought patterns in order to enable healthy choices in the context of larger system awareness.

Whom Do We Serve?

Meg Wheatley

One thing that interests me is something you've mentioned, Bob. Whom do we serve, as OD practitioners? For myself, I have always been interested in what was going on with people inside of the system. But I am personally committed to encouraging people to notice this question of "Whom do you serve?" Is it our careers, our status, our paychecks, or people (the humanistic values)? Is it these deeper values? Is it some deeper recognition that a human being, whoever he or she is, is worth being active for?

We must realize what's happening inside organizations. We're no longer able to align humanistic values with economic values. That's what I mean when I say we lost. So for me the task now is for a lot of personal introspection about what it is that will really give me a valuable life. Am I only going to serve the economy and bring down the planet, or make a stand and figure out how I can serve the human spirit?

Bob Tannenbaum

This is important. It was very typical in those early years when most of us were university-based and had a guaranteed income that people entered the field to change the world. I'd ask interns what attracted them to the field, and the almost universal answer was, "I want to make this a better world. I want to have a role in improving the kind of world we're in." I think that has changed, at least for some.

Meg Wheatley

I believe that, starting in the 1930s, we made that disastrous split to create personnel functions so that line managers didn't have to worry about people. From that time onward, I have seen in the field of OD that we have been trying to recreate or reconnect this very dangerous split—between thinking that management is one set of skills and managing the organization is another set of skills, and that you don't have to do them both simultaneously.

It's disconcerting to feel that we may have, as a profession, created this imprisonment, these chains of ownership. We may feel that because we are working for the big consulting firms we aren't empowered to speak the truth as we see it. That becomes easier as we get older for sure. I have a great need for people who come into this field to ask themselves why they are really in it. Because if you're just in it for the money, there are easier ways to earn a living, right?

I was thinking that many in the field now have a different master than they had intended. They are restricted because of economic means or the desire to have a good life, a material advantage. And that's actually the same problem that's affecting the whole world right now. We are living in a time when the systems that started out as fairly benign (or at least more reasonable) have changed. Now everything is a slave to the economy. Everything is justified now by whether it helps the economy or it doesn't help the economy. The decision question is, "Is this going to give me the income I want?"

Bob Tannenbaum

Besides income, I think power and its attainment motivates an awful lot. Really, most of the politicians keep making decisions in terms of what it takes to be reelected. So apart from money, this need to hold on to power is pretty important.

A footnote to what you've been saying: I've been increasingly aware that what we now say is relevant not only to OD practitioners, but to all of the people who are facilitators—counselors, teachers, parents, and other consultants focused on process. If we're thinking about having an influence in society, there are many other practitioners who can also be relevant. The way of being effective with others is quite similar in these diverse roles.

John Adams

When we are talking about whom we serve, or what, my service is to the highest level my spiritual practices can take me. At the present, this means focusing on the greatest good, even in the darkest corners.

Kristine Quade

I determine whom I serve from the vantage point of agreements. First, I have agreements with myself about the kind of person I am (values and beliefs). Second, I have agreements about the kind of work that I will do (principles or guidelines).

With the first two agreements, I must be as clear as possible in order to enter a conscious agreement with the client. This goes to what others have said about knowing thyself, the self is the instrument, and knowing the reason I do my work. When I am unclear about my foundation, then I will fail to optimize the service I am to provide.

Julie DiBenedetto

I believe we as OD/HSD professionals are serving the individual, community, and organizational stakeholders that comprise the human systems from which they (and we) are a part. By "serving," I mean to help stakeholders to help themselves. Human Systems includes the word human, which implies everything associated with being human—mind, body, and spirit.

Carole Lyles Shaw

Fundamentally, I know that I serve my own values and interests. That's why clarity and self-awareness are such critical competencies for people in the helping fields. Secondly, I serve the people who create the economic value—that is, the folks who actually do the day-to-day work in my client systems.

To that end, I serve managers—the front-line supervisor, the team leader, the executive. I truly believe that skilled and caring managers create livable work environments, and it is my life work to help each manager do that job better and, as a consequence, experience more fulfillment in his or her own life as a result. I also believe that this pathway leads to viable organizations (for-profit, non-profit, government, and others). I do not believe that every organization should last forever—they never have in human history. So my work is *not* predicated on the assumption that the leader's work is to ensure that the organization survives.

Patty Sadallah

The "whom do we serve" question has always been two-pronged for me. There is the "client" and his or her best interests as a direct "who," but there is also an indirect beneficiary, a broader "whom." I choose the first very carefully and make sure that what they are about is consistent with what I am all about.

When I worked with my first non-profit client, I was totally hooked! I prefer working with client systems that really care about the mission and outcomes for their client communities. It is rewarding to work in the community development area and be able to sit back and see stronger neighborhoods and know that, in a small way, I helped.

Andrea Sigetich

I attempt to always serve the individual who has appeared in front of me. I believe that serving—I mean really serving—the individual will serve the community and, ultimately, the world.

Richard Axelrod

I believe the answer to the question about service is that we serve everyone. We serve those who are in front of us in the moment when we attend to them, and we serve those who are not there when we ask ourselves how this will impact those who are not present. We serve those whose voices are in the room when we listen attentively and those whose voices are not in the room when we bring their concerns into the conversation. We serve our self-interest when we place our values or our economic needs first and the self-interest of others as we facilitate their agendas.

We serve those in power as we help make their dreams come true and those not in power when we help make their dreams come true. We serve the whole when we take the systems view, and we serve the part when we make sure they are included in the conversation. We serve those who have come before us and those who will come after us. In the words of Martin Buber, "We serve both I and thou."

Who we serve is a vast tapestry of clients and interests and who we serve in the moment is much like a Gestalt. And what we decide in the moment is who or what is foreground and what is background. Is our own or the client's self-interest foreground or background? Is the whole or the part foreground or background? Are our values or the client's values foreground or background? And it is how we answer those questions in the moment that seals our collective fate and determines who we serve and whether or not that service makes a difference.

• FREEZE FRAME

Now that you have read Chapter 1—addressing questions of identity, purpose, and service—consider your answers to the following questions before you move on to the next section.

1. Having considered the purposes that other OD professionals have talked about, how have your own thoughts about purpose evolved? Write a two-sentence description of your purpose in this field as you now see it.

2. Based on what you read about the field's identity, boundaries, overlaps, and conflicts, what would you like to learn about related fields, if anything? What do you believe professionals in this field should do to clarify the field's identity?

3. As you consider your original thoughts on whom you serve and the discussion here, how might you phrase a statement regarding whom you serve if a client asked it?

4. As you move to the next chapter—Principles in Action—consider the relationship of your purpose to your operating principles or values.

OUR STORIES

Throughout the book, we will offer brief stories of how some of the OD practitioners who participated in these conversations came to the field. This group entered the field because the values they perceived as core to this field fit with strongly held values of their own about the importance of social justice.

Bev Scott

My roots are similar to others of my generation. I came to OD from social action and social justice after working in the War on Poverty in the 1960s and being actively involved in anti-racism education in Detroit in the early 1970s. I found kindred spirits in this field who held the values of equity, participation, humane organizations, growth, and development. I also found I could apply my academic training in sociology and psychology, and I discovered the value of personal growth. The opportunity to learn about myself, to grow, and to develop insight and understanding was a special reward that I had not originally identified when I decided I wanted to "do OD."

William Gellermann

Ever since I can remember, my purpose (although I didn't know to call it that) was to make the world a better place. OD brought me to a clearer sense of how I might do that—by facilitating the development of organizations so they might better serve their purposes. But now I have found that most publicly chartered corporations are required by their charters to serve their stockholders, and that the courts have interpreted that to mean maximizing stockholder value in the short run. So now I'd like to join with others who are seeking to change corporate charters so they can serve all of their stakeholders, and my purpose has expanded to serving the global community. My particular focus is working with the United Nations and its network/community of human systems.

Mimi Weber

I began my career as an RN, although I had always thought about a career in education or counseling. In retrospect, the field of OD has given me the opportunity to do all the things that I love: bring healing to a situation that has created personal or organizational pain, facilitate learning and problem solving to promote personal and organizational growth, and continue on my own path of growth and development. I have always been passionate about helping others and making a difference, always wanted to work with compassion, empathy, creativity, and personal integrity. As an internal consultant, OD gives me the chance to do that on a daily basis.

Thomas C. Matera

When I first discovered OD as a coherent field that one could practice as a profession, I was searching for a way to help people improve their lives in the organizations they seemed so bound to. Today, my purpose remains the same, although I now call it seeking personal and social justice (and I don't think people are quite so "bound" to the organization as they were in 1982). There is no way to peace; peace is the way: in ourselves, in our organizations, in our culture, and in our world. I know no other profession whose incumbents so completely aspire to these achievements. That's why I got in; that's why I'm still here.

Matt Minahan

As a child of the 1960s, I was brought up to believe that I had only one job: to make the world better. I am daily aware that of the world's six billion people, 1.2 billion live on less than $1 a day, and that less than 1 percent of our federal budget goes to aid those countries affected by drought and flood and famine and sickness. I believe we are responsible to use our health and wealth and education to help these people. We have such uncountable blessings that I believe I have no choice but to give back to those who have less. That's what drew me to the field and keeps me in it today.

Julie A. DiBenedetto

I chose the field of OD as a profession because I knew the world could be a better place and I was (and still am) willing to do my part to help. I believe one person does make a difference in the development of the whole! There were those who thought I was foolish to leave my "well-paying" position with "upward mobility" for the opportunity to dedicate my career to facilitating the development of human systems. Yet, I knew (and still know) this path is my life purpose as well as career purpose.

Principles in Action

• FREEZE FRAME

In this chapter we consider the role of values and principles in our practices. Take a few minutes to consider your thoughts on the questions below before beginning this chapter.

1. Reflect on the principles and values that guide your work. What are they?

2. How have your principles and values guided the type of work you accept and how you do your work?

3. How have your principles and values been challenged in your work?

4. How have you resolved those challenges?

5. What messages or questions about operating principles and values do you have for other practitioners?

6. To what extent should OD practitioners be neutral facilitators helping others through change and to what extent should they serve as activists of their principles? Why?

• • •

Principles in Action

Bob Tannenbaum

A central focus throughout my career has been on the individual. I have sometimes used the phrase "the centrality of the individual"—but in using that phrase I don't mean an isolated individual. "That which is human" would come closer. Even my team building was focused more on the individual and the relationships within the team than it was on problem solving. I figured, if I could make headway on the human side, that doing so would have a positive impact on their process. This focus has involved me sometimes in an inner conflict when I'm working in an organization where there are organizational issues that, at first glance, seem to be more technical than human.

My central focus came to me at an early age when I had my first encounter with anti-Semitism when I was in about the third grade. A bunch of fellows followed me home from school and taunted me. I could see their venom, the hatred, the nastiness, and it was terrifying. It seemed so unfair, so inhuman, to treat another human being this way.

Meg Wheatley

Bob, your experience reminds me of a really big question: "What do any of us believe the human spirit is? How would you define it?" Right now I would answer by saying that the human spirit is essentially creative, is essentially relational, and is essentially free. Those three things, being creative, relational, and free, are things that I learned in biology as the nature of all life. All of life must be free to choose. It will never just obey. So freedom becomes an essential force.

When I'm in organizations, I see so many of the practices, the routines, and the mechanisms we use to control people in use because we don't think well of ourselves as a species. We think, maybe *we* are creative, but everybody else is not. Maybe *we* are trustworthy, but most employees are not. Maybe *we* are open to change, but nobody else is. It's been a very important question to me, to keep asking people, "What do you believe to be true about human nature?" I also ask, "Is the behavior congruent with the belief?"

Francis (Frank) M. Duffy

Thank you Bob and Meg. I would go another step by saying I'm not an idealist. I'm an "idea-builder," an "architect of conceptual designs," and I dislike theory that cannot be applied in practice. I guess this is my way of saying that I prefer operational values. Operational values that make sense to me include

1. Work hard not to harm my client;
2. Provide services based on what my client needs or wants, rather than on what I want to do;
3. Do not foist my personal social or moral values on my client;
4. Tell the truth;
5. Confront wrongdoing (corruption, cheating, lying); and
6. Build my client's capacity to improve without my assistance.

I guess managers could substitute the word "employees" for "client" and the values might still work. These values are for me, not for my clients. Those are my marching orders, not my clients' orders. These values put a frame around my behavior, not around my clients' behaviors. Thus, I tell the truth, but I don't force my clients to accept that value.

I confront wrongdoing when I see it, but I don't force my clients to confront wrongdoing when they see it. None of the values I listed prevents me from telling a client what I think of his or her behavior. For goodness sake, those of you who know me know full well that I am more than willing to tell you what I think and feel:-). But all of those personal values prevent me from expecting my clients to think, feel, and act like I do.

So if I see a client's behavior as immoral or illegal, I tell the truth and point that out. And I point out the consequences of that wrongdoing. But I then don't turn around and say to a client, "Okay, from now on you *must* never again do anything wrong because that violates *my* values."

I believe that my clients are entitled to their personal values, beliefs, choices, and opinions. But if they choose to live by those things and if those things have negative affects, then those clients are simultaneously entitled to the consequences. Every choice has a consequence—sometimes negative, sometimes positive. "Make a choice, live by the consequences" is a motto that frames my life.

Hank Karp

Let me add a story I call "Lessons Learned from a Dead Lizard." Some years ago, my parents had retired to Miami. Whenever I went to visit them, I spent as much time as I could stretched out on the sand, no more than twenty-five feet from the water. One afternoon, in my fourth hour of baking in the sun, I looked up and noticed a small lizard hanging onto the toe thong of my leather sandal. He was about two and a half inches long, had lost his tail, had a scar down his back, and had, what looked like to me, a black eye. Now this was assuredly the most pathetic, beat-up lizard ever to grace the face of the earth.

Since I am an OD consultant and a member of the support professions, all my instincts to help came immediately to the surface. If I didn't get this little lizard out of the sun and back to the vegetation, he would surely die. Thus I decided to transport him over the hot sand to a cool palm grove next to the snack bar.

I picked up my sandal very gently and started the trek barefoot. I had to walk very slowly so as to avoid jarring him off the sandal over sand hot enough to qualify me for instant manhood in any primitive tribe on the planet. The upside was that the pain I had to endure made the act all that more noble.

When I finally reached the grove, I very carefully set the sandal down in the shade of some shrubbery and, feeling very good about myself, stepped back to see what would happen. The small lizard hung onto the thong for a few moments and then, very gingerly, looking both ways, stepped down to the ground—whereupon a large lizard came out of the shrubbery and ate him.

I remember going through four emotional reactions very quickly. First was horror. HORROR! Second was anger—at the large lizard for eating my client and at the small lizard for allowing himself to be eaten. Third was sadness, some for the untimely demise of the lizard and a lot for the negative outcome of what was really a very nice piece of work on my part. Finally came the philosophical adjustment of, "What the hell, win some lose some."

It wasn't until some time later that the real message of what happened dawned on me. Not only wasn't I the poor un-thanked, unappreciated hero of the piece, I was the villain!! Once aware of this, four things occurred to me. First, it had taken the lizard a much longer time to get to a place of relative safety, where I found him, than it took for me to take him back. Second, what I endured made absolutely no difference, whatsoever, to the outcome. Third, at no time did the lizard ever say to me, "Hey, Hank, do you want to give me a hand here?" The fourth, and by far the most important revelation . . . I had assumed that I knew what was best for the lizard!

This incident really did get me to think about my role as an OD consultant and to challenge some of the principles of effective support that I had been taught and had evolved myself. Below is a list of the guidelines that I now espouse and that have assisted me in becoming what I hope is a more effective supporter of individual and organizational growth:

1. Avoid taking responsibility for others; it isn't yours.

2. Avoid giving advice . . . opinion, on the other hand, is fine.

3. Focus on what's going well with the client as well as the problem . . . it provides needed balance and facilitates self-support.

4. Do nothing for the client that she is capable of doing herself. To do other than this promotes dependency.

5. Don't protect people from yourself. If your client is doing something self-destructive and you do not share your anger, you are colluding with the act.

6. Support the stronger; work with the weaker. Don't kill or weaken the driving force. Rather, help others to learn how to cope with it and become driving forces themselves.

7. Focus on the choice, not the action. I don't want the weaker to always confront the stronger. I want the weaker to generate choices and then to choose what is the best choice for *right now*.

8. Provide empathy, not sympathy. Sympathy says, "Poor baby, I feel what you feel." This is nonsense and reinforces the "victim" role. Empathy says, "I understand what you feel" and provides a bond for solid support.

9. Encourage selfness, aggression, and arrogance. WAIT! WAIT! Let me define my terms. *Selfness:* I get what I want and I exploit nobody. *Aggression:* Actively pursuing what you want from the environment. *Arrogance:* Supreme confidence in one's self-worth. Not such bad stuff when viewed from this perspective.

10. Take care of yourself first. If you happen to be the client's sole source of support in the moment, by taking care of yourself first you (1) become a model for appropriate behavior, (2) are the first to sense danger or an inappropriate path about to be taken, and (3) are actually guarding your client's sole source of support.

Who knows, perhaps the lizard died for a higher cause.

Matt Minahan

There's another lesson implicit in your cautionary tale, Hank: There will always be unintended consequences and, sometimes, they will be my fault. That doesn't make me bad or incompetent; it makes me human. And the better job I do of being human, the better job I'll do of being a good consultant.

Edward Hampton

I agree with Frank Duffy's list and endorse it. I would like to modify one of his items and add three more, however. To his "do my client no harm," I would simply say "Do no harm."

To explain why I think this is an important distinction, I need to add my first additional principle: OD should be done systemically or with a systems frame. No organization, person, or process operates independently. All is part of a complex network of intertwined relationships. I think that when OD is more harmful than helpful, a probable root cause will be that the OD consultant's view was too narrow. So, as one issue was fixed, it exacerbated another.

I think that when a manager or leader is "in the trenches," it is hard to maintain perspective. It is easy to become myopic and develop tunnel vision. A good consultant who is able to think systemically can help develop and maintain broad perspective and, in so doing, probably reduce the chance of doing harm inadvertently. So I say, "Do no harm." Think about the system and make sure all of the stakeholders are equally considered when preventing harm.

A second principle I would add is that OD should be done *empathically*. I like what Hank Karp says about empathy, but I would go further. I would say that empathy is the ability to see the reactions your actions will create before they happen so you can avoid those that will create harm. Empathy is the ability to exhibit great emotional intelligence and, I think, is a key to meeting the mandate to do no harm.

A third principle I would add is that an OD person is *competent*. In my view, a key ingredient of competence is having models and theories to apply. I am fond of saying anyone can "do OD." However, not everyone can do *OD consulting*. That takes a special skill set. I think an OD consultant who is professional is one who has been schooled and armed with enough models and theory to be able to competently and effectively deal with a wide array of organizations.

Jim Smith

I am amazed with how this conversation ties with the work of Abraham Maslow, who, in *The Psychology of Being* and *The Furthest Reaches of Human Nature,* describes his search for health in people, organizations, and society. He emphasizes again and again that vast pools of creativity exist deeper in organizations than many people believe. His exploration of the "peak experience" embraces the discussion of spirit and higher consciousness. Maslow asks:

> "What are the factors that make it possible for healthy people to perceive reality more efficiently, to predict the future more accurately, to perceive more easily what people are really like? What are the factors that make it possible for these people to endure or to enjoy the unknown, the unstructured, the ambiguous, and the mysterious? Why do the wishes of healthy people have so little power to distort their perceptions? The healthier people are, the more these capacities are interrelated."

I think early T-group experiences produced peaks for people, as they often left in euphoria and trembled to think of going home after having been transformed on some level. Sometimes it was the first time people got present with others, and often this was the result of the experience of having others truly present with them.

Jeff McCollum

I have just jiggled loose some ideas that have been tucked away but were learned in the process of coping (and helping an organization cope) with a major change created by Pfizer's acquisition of Warner-Lambert a few years ago.

The principle that I strive to apply—both as an OD consultant and a manager of others—is service. I don't mean service in the sense of the "customer is always right" or in the sense of submerging my own independence to clients. I mean it in the sense of conducting myself in a way that serves others by helping them learn and grow. As a consultant, it implies transferring what I know to the client and client system and, if correctly applied, requires that I not collude with the power structure in the organization. In individual coaching, it requires helping the person with whom I am working to grow and learn to the point where he or she can help others grow and learn by developing competence, confidence and, if needed, compassion.

In medieval days, the "fool" was the person who could tell the truth to the king. In a sense, OD practitioners can/should be the contemporary equivalents of the fool.

Geoff Bellman

I realize because of this conversation that there is a small bag of assumptions I carry into each new consulting relationship. I don't think of them so much as principles as just "what I do." But I do return to these considerations over and over again—especially when starting new consulting relationships.

My first consideration is that I pay more attention to the client and less to the work. Most of the time the presenting work is not what we end up doing as consultants. I am more interested in answering the questions, "Is this a person I can work with? Is there potential for our work relationship? Does this have potential for a long-term friendship?" I know the work will change, so I want to begin to build a stable, trusting relationship with the client. So I propose to talk to others as a way of gathering quick information. The work has begun. I want to quickly dive into the organization, and I want the client to experience a benefit right away.

My second consideration is that my client and I are two individuals pursuing our life work through the work we do. I seek connection with others who are engaged in their life purpose through the work that is being done. I assume that people are doing the best they know how. I do not arrive expecting they are screwed up and need to do things differently. Instead, I believe they are likely well-intentioned and need to do some things differently. Often, they need to use their present abilities in new ways. I help them *see* their world differently, allowing them to *do* their work differently. I have positive expectations of people and am often right.

My third consideration is that I approach the client positively, looking for the opportunity to work together. Since I limit the work I do, I also am deciding if I will do *this* work. I seek to understand what the client is talking about because my principle is that I have a deep respect for people, regardless of viewpoint. Their viewpoints deserve respect and honor and my attention. They honor me in sharing intimate information about the organization. With this, I am living out one of the unique OD perspectives around the belief in human potential. I hope to live it out in small but consistent ways.

I believe people do what they do for good reasons. If what they are doing is wrong or not the best choice, they still do it out of good reason. They have not ended up in their current predicament because they gave it no thought. No, this isn't always true, but it is that assumption I arrive with.

Robert Marshak

I believe that people operate out of their own level of reality or consciousness, which means everyone has learned particular ways of seeing and experiencing the world. These ways of seeing and experiencing lead to how people interpret and respond in any particular circumstance. Because I come from the premise that if people had a different way of looking at the world they would have a different way of behaving in the world, a primary intervention for me is to somehow try to reframe reality.

A key step before working with others is that I have to be clear and grounded in who I am and my values, ethics, and principles. I should also add that the act of being able to claim oneself, to claim one's own identity, is the single most powerful thing one can do, as opposed to living out the identity or reality imposed or suggested by parents, authority figures, and/or society.

Unfortunately, for many, to spend time on discovering and owning "who I am" is the willful act of a selfish person. The act of claiming oneself, claiming one's own true identity, is opposite to what we are often taught about serving others: to put others' needs and wants and issues first. The magic for dealing with a client or client system is that it starts with my own clarity about me, who I am, and how I can use that to work with the realities of others.

My work as a consultant is to discover that reality or consciousness or to "find, form, and frame reality." Consequently, I am always trying to figure out or learn the reality of others, to be able to see the world the way they do. As I enter a client system, I ask myself, "Given what they are saying (and doing in front of me), is it possible for them to achieve the results they want within their current reality and consciousness?" If the answer is "yes," I proceed within their current reality. If the answer is "no," I immediately begin to "test" the possibilities for changing the reality or consciousness of the client or client system. Sometimes this is nothing more than some comments or observations made during contracting. Sometimes it is a specific "intervention." What I seek to do is to consciously reframe how something is conceived in order to determine whether or how change can occur.

My sad moments are when I have taken an assignment and for whatever reasons compromised my true values or ignored the usual warning signs because I wanted to work with "that client," wasn't really thoughtful about what I was doing, or thought I "needed the money." My happy moments are when the client or client system sees things in a new way or experiences something in a way that permits new ways of dealing with the world or realizing new opportunities that seemed impossible a few moments before. It feels even better when they know I was somehow involved but ultimately felt the change was because of them rather than because of me. That, of course, is contributing to their ability to claim their own identity and reality and to understand the power of choice in how to engage and deal with others and the world.

Meg Wheatley

For me the task now is for a lot of personal introspection about what it is that will really give me a valuable life. As I mentioned earlier, I think we've lost the battle of humanistic values versus economic values. And we're continuing to lose it, unless we redefine what our role is now. It's true not only for the field of OD; I feel it's true for leaders, public school teachers, and people in healthcare.

John Agno

Meg, I agree. Transpersonal psychologist and psychiatrist Roger Walsh, author of *Essential Spirituality,* tells us that for the first time in human history every single one of our global problems is human-created. Every one is a reflection of our individual and collective choices and behavior. And this means that the state of the world is a reflection of the state of our minds.

It is everyone's personal choice to become aware and to take action on our guiding principles at work, at home, and throughout the world.

Diana Whitney

That connects with the theories of social science around the premise that the concept of objectivity does not exist. Instead there is a social construction that "something becomes as we observe it." To observe something, we need to call attention to it. What we call attention to is what we focus people's attention on. We are always in a position to be influencing, and because of that we need to have a consciousness about what we are influencing, especially through the questions we ask.

I believe we are currently advocates because the old models and theories implied objectivity. My operating principle is that social realities are created and held in the language of relationship. For example, I believe that poverty is a broken relationship. Wherever there is poverty of intellect, finances, or equality, there is something that is not fulfilling that needs to be brought back in relationship with people.

We don't change anything; all we do is preserve what we care about.

Stan Herman

I find myself realizing that I have not asked myself about my own principles for a long time. And when I ask it of myself now, I find that I have very few—perhaps even none. It's not that I never had any. I have had, as a matter of fact, several complete sets. When I was a young, fast-tracking, hot-blooded manager in a big corporation, my principles were about clear-cut, right-doing codes of ethics. For example, I once had a loud argument with a senior executive to keep him from cutting off a worker's pension. (I won.)

When I was a mid-career consultant to senior managers, my principles were about helping my client to get a clear idea of what he really wanted and then helping him to recognize his available options. As a more senior (I really mean older) consultant, my values were similar to many I see above, especially Hank Karp and Frank Duffy. I agree with Meg. What happened? Where have all the principles gone?

Best I can figure, I don't think that things like principles and values have much actual impact on what people do anymore. Perhaps they once did, but in these times laws and regulations (with sanctions) rule. So what I do pretty much is to ask myself what kind of a guy am I, and am I likely to run amok without restraints? My answer to myself is that basically I'm a pretty good guy and, no, I'm not likely to do anyone much harm if they haven't harmed me. But what, I then ask myself, if they do harm me? I guess I'll have to wait until that happens before I can tell.

For me the best principles are those that do not have a predetermined righteousness but rather an openness to new possibilities. For example, a value of mine that seems to have emerged for now is "to continue to expand and extend my perspectives." When I expand my perspectives, I see more of the landscape—a broader range of possibilities and options from which to choose the actions of my life. When I extend my perspectives, I see my purpose and destiny—the connections between the actions of my life and the operation of its divine plan. Maybe this one will change too.

David Hock Wang Heng

I have been grappling with the notion of vulnerability. As a line manager, especially in a command and control hierarchy (law enforcement), oftentimes I have to appear to be on top of the situation. However, I know better how much I do not know. The need to make others think I am competent drains my energy. At the same time, I have seen moments of enlightenment when others are drawn to engage in a different conversation with me when they discover my softness. One learning I have attempted to pursue is whether it is possible to lead from a position of weakness.

My primary value of engagement in relationships is to reflect on what I am learning about myself. Perhaps this is what Stan refers to as the range of perspectives. Sometimes I find myself seething with anxiety to be helpful so as to control my fear of rejection. Unlike many of the more experienced people in this discussion thread, I find that I am a novice in being able to confront emotional tensions. At the same time I wonder whether this is going to be a lifelong journey.

Chuck Phillips

My simplistic view is to remember that all organizations are collections of individuals. Like Geoff Bellman, I have a strongly held belief that, at the core, virtually everyone is trying to do the best that he or she can. (Thank you, Sid Simon, who once said, "No one gets up in the morning, looks in the mirror, and says, 'Today I'm going to be a shithead!'") A part of this is believing that people know what is "right" and that, given an environment that seeks, encourages, and supports that, people will act on their view of "rightness."

John Adams

I was recently asked how I "held" my work, and I blurted out without thinking that I try to support people in growing into their full "space." I didn't really have a clue what I meant by that and was unable to immediately answer the inevitable next question, "What does that mean?" After a few moments of thought, I replied that the biggest impact of being in this field is developing my voice, my presence, and my courage—and I guess that's what I meant by helping people "fill their space." And as I reflect on my various work arenas, I have always called forth these qualities in others as well.

Richard Axelrod

I loved Francis Duffy's list of values and Hank Karp's (lizard) principles. I love principles because they help guide me when I don't know what to do in facing a new challenge or situation. The problem with principles is there are so many of them. Which ones do you choose? Which ones do you make part of your practice?

A number of years ago, I was a part of a meeting with a number of other creators of different large-group interventions. The purpose was to develop a unifying set of principles. We discussed each other's principles in order to discover the foundational elements of each other's work. Then we tried to identify the principles we held in common, but that was a less than satisfying experience because, although it produced common ground, it was too bland. Each of us felt some eternal truth was missing.

Finally someone said, "It's like dogs and their owners." Each of us had developed a methodology that was explained by a subsequent set of principles because of who we are, and, to a large extent, our methodologies were a product of who we were in the world and our experience as human beings. Some principles that were front and center in one methodology were background or assumed in another methodology. Yet when you looked at the whole, they were all there.

I think there is a process that begins with the reading about a principle or creating your own principle and saying, "Yes, I want to adopt that principle and make it my own." I could take any of the principles in this discussion and say, "Yes, that is a great principle," but it is only when I try to apply that principle that I come to grips with what that principle really means, what it really stands for. It is the crucible of application that makes the difference between giving lip service to the principle and making it your own. It is through the struggle I experience applying the principle to myself and others that I develop a deeper understanding of what it stands for and how to work with it. And as a consequence of that struggle, of dealing with its truths and ambiguities, I become a better practitioner.

David Szymanowski

I believe that our profession is part science, part craft, and part art. We need to keep each straight in our discussions. As a scientist, some type of philosophy of science and epistemology guides us. Our scientifically based tools tend to be our commonality. To varying degrees, each of us has facility with other specialty tools: financial, human relations, computer systems, organizational designs, cultural sensitivities, and the like. System modeling, learning as communities, and collaborating are still yet examples of other unique tools. The craft is in knowing which tools to use, when to use them, where to use them, and how to use them. The craft is in becoming an expert with the tools in our toolbox. As a craftsperson, some form of principles guide us. Up to this point, it is part science and part craft.

Organization development is a people-intensive and people-valued enterprise mingled with many unknowns and myriad ways to cope with these unknowns, unexpected storms, frequent undiscussables, unintended consequences, and stones strewn about. Using these raw materials and his or her personality, the change merchant weaves his or her artistry of change. Guided by a particular shuttle of scientific philosophy, the change merchant co-projects a vision from the mind's eyes onto a particular organization's loom and weaves into this yet-to-be fabric a particular body of knowledge and organizational methods, interleaving experienced and expert crafting of systems. The fabric created will be tough enough and flexible enough to sustain the wear of time and political battles. It will be beautiful and useful enough not to gather dust in a mausoleum of dated manuscripts.

The change merchant will be gracious enough to facilitate fruitful communication, practical and sharp enough to be useful and timely, sensitive enough to be humane, robust enough to make the journey, farsighted enough to plan ahead, wise enough to seek guidance, humble enough to work on other people's dreams, caring enough to honor liberty and diversity, close enough to be creative, distant enough not to be enmeshed, savvy enough to survive alternate realities, and occasionally swift enough to flee.

Even though it is an infant profession, ethics guide and principles inform us. I strive to have the organization vision of an eagle, the tenacity of a bulldog, and watchful caring of an organizational shepherd.

Frederick A. Miller

This has been informative to understand how other practitioners reconcile, integrate, or separate their personal principles and their work. Like many people here, I feel that my values guide all areas of my life, including the work I do with clients. It would, therefore, be inconsistent to set my values aside when working in an organization, or worse yet, to deny my personal principles. My values are deeply connected to my identity as an African American man raised in the inner city of Philadelphia. I take that background and that community with me wherever I go.

Oppression and "isms" are present everywhere, and a large part of what motivates me is reducing and eliminating their impact. I equate "neutrality" about values with collusion. What I have decided to do with my life (in my work and beyond) is to use my voice—as well as my knowledge and influence—to resist and defeat those "isms."

It makes no sense to me to compartmentalize my principles in any way, and so I bring my values—my bias, my agenda—unabashedly to my work. I do this through my writings, conference presentations, initial contracting with clients, and throughout my work with clients. As a result, they have a clear sense of what they are getting up-front. This may indeed be a deal-breaker for some clients. If their values and mine coincide, or if their goal is to create an environment that mirrors my values, we are a match. If not, so be it. At any rate, it should be clear to them that they are hiring me for my values and that, while other elements may be negotiable (like timing, intensity, positioning, timeframe, and maybe even spin), the values themselves are not. They are central to my work.

One reason I take this approach is that I don't think of my role as a "helper" to my clients. I find something self-aggrandizing and paternalistic in that term. I am not their hero or their savior. I am a partner in a mutually beneficial relationship. They want to change their culture; I have knowledge and talent around making that happen. Together we create a vision of where the organization needs to be and then examine where they are (their current state) and the ways in which they are failing to live up to that vision (their aspired-to state). We create strategies for living that vision. A large part of what I do is hold them accountable, through our partnership, to moving toward their vision and living their values.

This is substantially different from my "leading" the client or merely accepting the agenda they lay out (or revise along the way) without making qualitative judgments about it. In a way, everything I do is a value judgment that is grounded in my principles. In this sense, our values and principles are the most fundamental tools an OD practitioner has.

Edith Seashore

I support what you are saying, Fred, because I also believe our set of values will impact the client from the very beginning. For example, data collection will always have some subjectivity based on the questions we ask or do not ask.

We should not initiate the values we hold, but we can share our points of view. We must make sure we are not the client or the driver of change. That is the client's job. When we are hired, they should know what we believe and what role we will play. If I am not in accord with the belief system, then I am not a good consultant for this client. They may not be acting in a style I prefer, or they may be operating from lack of information. I can become an advocate in seeking involvement and investment by the organization and its leaders. I can advocate that the bonus structure be tied to the success of the change effort because I know that there is commitment when money is tied to incorporating something new.

Bob Tannenbaum

My experience is that the OD learners have been motivated by a desire to make this a better world. This has a people implication rather than a technology implication, such as building a better car. The attraction to the field is because practitioners want to make a difference.

The toughest inner conflict we get into is when we are dealing with firms that are economically driven and need to survive by cutting costs or face going further into the negative. We, as OD people, feel a real conflict because we think in human terms, which is central to us. We find that reality is not consistent with our dream and are also forced to confront our own business at a time when we are getting fewer clients, less billable time, and are in a personal crunch. We find that our own decisions are made in terms of personal interests as well.

Becky DeStefano

What Bob and Edie are saying connects to the foundational personal principles that I use to guide my work, including honesty, love, listening, staying "clean" (not working my personal agenda), and helping people at all levels of the organization discover and do what's good for all the organization. So I have turned down some work: where the manager is sure he/she knows the answer and is trying to hire me to collude with him or her, where someone is being set up to take a fall, or work that includes a performance management system based on faulty assumptions.

I can remember a client I had fifteen years ago who, as part of the management group, continued to make condescending remarks about the employees' ability to contribute to the change—to even understand the problems to begin with. He kept saying things like, "All they are going to tell us (in data collection) is that they want fewer hours and a microwave in the lunchroom." In my best self-serving memory of the incident, I believe I asked questions in an attempt to encourage others in the group to confront him so we could move on. Unfortunately, he had perceived power in the group and continued to dominate.

I finally asked my primary client's permission to leave the job. In that case, my own philosophical position made it impossible to engage in a way that was totally free from bias. As a more mature professional today, I'm sure there were ways of handling the situation that didn't include me giving up the work, but damn if I could think of any of them the day I walked out.

Patricia Firestone

Since I am currently functioning as an internal consultant to one of the largest fire departments in the United States, I may have a different experience.

One of my initial efforts, at the behest of the fire chief, was to facilitate the construction of a vision for the department and to identify the organization's core values. As a female, civilian, and outsider, I was greatly challenged as the work took place over the next year to make this happen in an organization whose tradition was dominated by "insiders" who are white males in blue collars. To my clients' surprise, and mine, we have grown to value and even treasure the differences between us. Our differing points of view enrich the decision making taking place within a traditional command-and-control structure.

Roselyn Kay

A consultant's role is one from which we have or can be assumed to have a certain level of power and influence and afforded great trust that we will keep a group, organization, or individual safe. How we use that can be wonderful or disastrous. My principles of "ferocious caring" guide me:

- *Fairness:* to be fair in all my deals with individuals or organization leadership because I value people being fair with me

- *Expectation:* to expect much from others (people often rise to the level we expect)

- *Respect:* to demonstrate respect of people in order to get respect

- *Ownership:* to take ownership for my "stuff" when dealing with others and when making a commitment

- *Courage:* to have the courage to say no to things that are against my values and principles even if it costs me financially. In other words, when will my "no" be meaningful if I don't say it?

- *Integrity:* to work with integrity and expect the same from others

- *Opportunity:* to be aware of opportunities that exist for me and others to do our best work, and live our best life

- *Understanding:* to demonstrate understanding in all interactions and learning

- *Spirituality:* hold deep respect for the connections in all things

- *Courage:* to try something new, to say no, to say yes, to take risks

- *Authenticity:* to be true to myself at work and home

- *Recognize:* myself often and others more—to give credit where credit is due

- *Intellect:* keep abreast of information needed to be excellent and to help others achieve

- *Nurture:* to be a good listener; nurturing family, friends, clients, and anyone else who needs support

- *Graceful:* to be gracious with others and graceful when working with others

Here I would have to ask myself to what extent I am willing to compromise elements of my "ferocious caring" in order to work with those who have differing values. That would depend on whether the request for my expertise allowed me to operate still using my gifts while maintaining my integrity and respect for self and others. Diversity is a beautiful thing if one opens the mind to other ways of being, doing, living!

Bev Scott

I have grown my values. They have their roots in the values my parents passed on: to respect and look for the best in others, to seek learning and challenges, to make a contribution and give something back, to appreciate nature and its wonder. As my own life has unfolded, additional values have become important to me, such as equity and justice, participation and having a voice, peace, respecting the perspective, culture, and values of others.

These personal values are embedded in my professional values as well as the work I do with clients to support their growth and to develop organizations that will do the same. I also find that I must hold the paradox of conflicting values, especially when others' cultures and values conflict with my values of equity and justice or having a voice. I have learned that I must continue to examine what values are important so that they stay present and provide guidance.

Valerie Wallen

I live from and thrive on the core principles of *freedom* and *accountability*. The rich meaning and challenging process of acting out these concepts are what motivates me. By that, I mean that I have not arrived in "mastering." I never want to treat my core values as if I have "arrived," and I yearn to grow into all the many facets of their rich meanings and expressions.

I work to free up the flow of information and the relevance and validity of the information that flows. I desire to integrate this authenticity of information in the everyday act of supporting the freedom of personal choice for myself and others. With this authenticity, we move beyond masks into honesty and trust. In order to maintain this level of honesty and trust, I strive to facilitate a freedom of choice that includes freedom from coercion.

If my values seem too basic or over-simplified, it is because I admit that I am on the initial end of my values learning curve. I have only been working from these principles for the last five years on any conscious level.

David Coghlan

Two things have come out of my encounter group experiences. One was my own personal development, and the second learning developed from the writings of Carl Rogers. I discovered an approach to helping that took as its basis the self-directive nature of the person and the role of the professional helper as one who facilitates the client's self-directedness.

Shortly afterwards I was introduced to OD and got excited by the process of using client-centered approaches to helping teams and organizations function, rather than focusing on individual personal growth.

At the core of OD is a genuine client-centeredness, which aims to release the potential in individuals to participate in organizations and teams. For me, critical to engaging in OD is some form of educational interventions that facilitate members of the systems with which I'm working to reflect on their experience and try to learn from them.

Anne Meda

As a manager leading highly technical work teams, I have developed guidelines or a code of conduct that reflects my own personal values. I have found it necessary to bring to the team's awareness certain values and behavioral aspects (such as conducting oneself with integrity, honesty, prudence, respect, wisdom, and so forth) with the purpose of fostering an environment that will teach people how to effectively work together as well as aid in their own personal growth. I have found this to create an environment of creativity (bringing forth excellent business solutions) and freedom (from criticism and judgment), which in turn creates very strong relational ties.

Glenda Eoyang

We think of ourselves as "values" driven, yet one of our values is valuing others' values. We catch ourselves in a conundrum in which we are individually bound to respect others' perspectives while, as a field, we are bound to define ourselves and our colleagues through a shared set of values. Values can emerge from the interactions across differences between participants in the system. Together, we use our histories, expectations, and understanding to engage with others around a specific concern, issue, or environment. Within the specific context, we work together for shared values to emerge. When we move to a new situation, we carry with us our expectations and learnings from our histories to engage in the next generation of values exchange and clarification. Engagements are not situational compromises. They are opportunities to sharpen our values on the whetstone of others' perspectives.

I use seven simple principles to help me shape patterns of productive interactions in human systems:

- Teach and learn in every interaction;

- Reinforce strengths of self and other;

- Search for the true and the useful;

- Apply emerging learnings in reflective practice;

- Make expectations explicit;

- Give and get value for value; and

- Attend to the whole, the part, and the greater whole.

Of course you can see how every traditional OD practice could easily conform to these principles. As I've shared these ideas with experienced professionals over the past few years, I've found that these dynamic assumptions reflect the intuitive practices of most of us. We know that individual learning determines and is determined by group transformation. We know that conversations among newcomers and old timers enrich both—and the field as a whole. We know that conversations about values are much more important than the values themselves. We know that no one technique is best for all situations. And we know that we cannot reliably predict the outcomes of our actions.

Bob Tannenbaum

It is amazing how I have learned to look at most events and interactions through the eyes of six basic notions. Three I'll discuss here, and the others I'll mention later. I am amazed at how timeless these notions are:

- Focus on systems thinking;

- Be rooted in values;

- Keep responsibility for change with the client;

- Be open and appropriately flexible;

- Be patient; deep change takes time; and

- Know thyself.

Be rooted in values: The nature of our personal values is deeply embedded in us from birth. Sometimes these values operate at an unconscious level, and our work is to become more aware of those personal values that drive the work we take and create the framework for how we conduct our engagements or how we advise our clients.

My underlying values relate to the centrality of human beings, who they are as people and their relationships with others. Both the human and organizational systems require relationships in order to stay connected as a system. Relationships are the glue of the system, and once their interdependencies are recognized, the more awareness there is of how the system is operating.

While the basic values of organization development—collaboration, cooperation, knowledge of self, social responsibility, and social justice—go a long way, there are a few more values that guide me in understanding deep change: humanism, authenticity, and timing. I believe I cannot be a whole human being unless I am authentic. Being authentic means that I am open as a system, without regard to the consequences. I am in my strength if I am true to who I am rather than playing to someone else in order to accomplish something.

Respect and understanding of timing as a value is rather tricky. The client system has its own timing. The individuals within the client system have their own timing. My authenticity also has its own timing. It is trust that brings everything together. Trust helps us to accurately be aware of what is going on in the system. The art of making the intervention appropriate and proactive is by testing the boundary of trust.

Be patient; deep change takes time: Surface level change can occur quickly; deep change takes an unbelievably long time. The deeper the change that is being faced, the closer the individual or organization comes to the center of the core identity, which is who I am. This type of change will involve the emotions, will, spirit, timing, trust, support, connection, authenticity, intentionality, purposefulness, tolerance for ambiguity, facing the unknown, anxiety, and more. When the system is ready to change, it will. In view of the slowness of deep change and healing with areas where change is deep, the central quality needed is patience, not planning!

Know thyself: The consultant is the carrier of the technique. As has been said by others in this conversation, we must be able to perceive accurately and then be able to act appropriately in light of our understanding of the situation. If there is a low awareness by the consultant of a tendency to misperceive or even block data, the result will be an effort that may miss the real issues.

I am convinced that if a person does not have a reasonably good knowledge of himself or herself, then our not knowing becomes our greatest enemy. It affects our perceptions, how we attach meaning to all the sensory input one receives and give meaning to the world that is out there. Not knowing ourselves affects how we diagnose and take action.

Getting to know oneself is a process. (Ha, there is that slow change again!) The self is a laboratory for learning, an individual system. My greatest friend is my feelings. I don't know what's going on unless I let my feelings tell me. Feelings are central to me and my whole process about learning about myself. My advice to all practitioners is to listen to your feelings—they are great consultants!

• FREEZE FRAME

Take a moment to answer the questions below as you reflect on what you have just read about how your colleagues in the field perceive their principles in action.

1. What new principles or values will you now add to those identified at the beginning of the chapter?

2. Ideas that you have for becoming more aware of your principles include . . .

3. If you had to limit your list of practice principles, what would your top four or five include?

4. How will you keep your principles or values before you as you work?

5. Ideas that you have for how you will react when your principles are challenged within certain systems include . . .

OUR STORIES

For the following group of practitioners, values centered on the individual and human potential were central to the reasons they were attracted to the field of OD.

Ed Hampton

As I do OD, I am strongly influenced and motivated by experiences that I had while serving in the Army. As a second lieutenant, I was supposedly ready to lead soldiers and organizations. I was not. Sometimes I still shudder from some of the mistakes I made. So when I do OD now, I carry a solemn and silent vow to help the potential victims of the incompetent. I want to help those with power and influence use that power wisely and competently so as not to cause harm from ignorance. So for me OD is a crusade of sorts, a holy cause to protect those who are not able to protect themselves.

Helene C. Sugarman

After almost twenty years as a theatre teacher, I left education. I've found a great similarity between mounting a theatre production and entering into a client system. In both activities, it's best to be collaborative, synergistic, and trusting of the process with an understanding that somehow together you and the client system will design a way of getting to your goals. Both systems are adjusting as you go with necessary corrections to keep on the path to the vision (one is artistic, the other organizational) and goals, with a selected strategy (which differs for each organization and each production). Now in OD I can access my creativity and continually practice another expression of my art.

Phil Nimtz

I came to OD through adventure training. As I look back, I can see that much of what we did was morale building more than team building. It didn't take long to realize that, while we had significant impact on some individuals and more rarely on whole teams, we could not begin to change the larger organizations in which these individuals and teams existed. My primary motivation is still the individuals and the ways they create meaning and value in their lives. I now realize that it is impossible to separate the individual from the organization or system.

Steve Cady

As a college student, I went through three different T-group experiences that lasted for two weeks each over the summer, followed by each group staying together for the rest of the summer working on student programming for the university. I got the bug and remember starting LEAD, Leadership Education and Development, as a program for students to come together in order to learn and grow. On the first night, over 150 students showed up. I remember holding a sheet of paper with the agenda behind my back because I was shaking so much. It was clear to me I was living my mission and I was scared $#!?less. And I was hooked on OD.

Roselyn Kay

I found my way to OD after over twenty-five years holding leadership positions in banking and finance. My responsibilities were driven by making the numbers—the focus was on financial results. However, I found that financial results were significantly enhanced by focusing on the people who so wonderfully used their strengths in service to the goals. Over time, I realized that my strengths included caring deeply about others' ability to find their passion and do their best work.

Deborah Arcoleo

I sort of "fell" into OD. I engineered a career change from management consulting to outplacement counseling and from that to starting and running an organizational consulting practice for the outplacement firm I worked for. I was looking for an opportunity to make a positive difference for people, and that remains my purpose today. The other part of my purpose is helping to make business organizations places where people can grow, learn, and find fulfillment—and maybe even have fun!

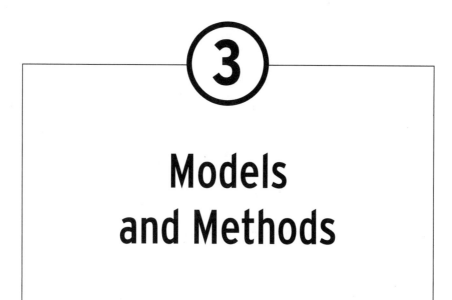

Models
and Methods

• FREEZE FRAME

Take a few minutes as you begin this chapter to consider your own answers to these questions.

1. What are the models that are the foundations of your work? Why?

2. What are the models and tools that have made a difference in your work or for your clients?

3. How have you adapted your favorite models? Why have those adaptations been important to you?

4. How do the models, methods, and tools you use, and the ways you adapt them, reflect your purpose in your work and the values that are core to you?

5. When you create your own models, what elements become important?

6. What advice would you give to a new practitioner regarding OD models and tools and their use?

•   •   •

OD Models and Methods

Bob Tannenbaum

As I mentioned earlier, I look at most events and interactions through the eyes of six basic notions. In a sense, they are my models and methods. Once again, they are

- Focus on systems thinking;

- Be rooted in values;

- Keep responsibility for change with the client;

- Be open and appropriately flexible;

- Be patient; deep change takes time; and

- Know thyself.

I talked about the values-related notions earlier. Here let me discuss several that I believe are basic to the way we operate in this field: focusing on systems thinking, keeping responsibility with the client, and being open and appropriately flexible.

Focus on systems thinking: Since everything is connected to or related to everything else, paying attention to the complexity of the system can cause overload. Therefore, it becomes easy to see only the presenting problem. If this becomes a focus, we may be blind to other aspects of the situation that might even be more important. Around every system there is a boundary. It was early learning about T-groups that helped me to see that there is a boundary or container for the T-group, such as time and space, but that anything can happen within the container because of the multitude of combinations of issues, individuals, reactions, and individual learning.

That helped me to look beyond the presenting problem to search for the interconnections that make up a larger system, the boundaries to the system, and the blocks or closures that are keeping the system from being healthy. This approach can be adapted to personal work, work with individuals, or work with groups and organizations.

Keep the responsibility for change with the client: Change agents seem to describe themselves as "the people who bring about change." I cannot think of any major organizational change that is brought about primarily by consultants. I don't think that it is our responsibility and certainly, ethically, it is not our position to "change the organization." I believe we are free to make suggestions, but the decision for change belongs to the person(s) who have the responsibility for the system (individual or organization). I have no right to make the decision of what changes ought to be made. I can introduce or open the dialogue, but it is the individual's responsibility to go ahead or not.

If I enter the system as the process facilitator and then start to sell my values or vision of the future, then I erode the trust foundation with the client. I have no agreement to operate from this platform. I have no problem with consultants being an advocate as long as they are clear they are being an advocate and the client is clear that they are being hired because of the particular views they hold. The difficulty is that the consultant becomes the architect of the change rather than the client, and failure is predictable.

How do I know this? Well, I don't believe many people or organizations have the tolerance to challenge their deep belief systems. It suggests instability, a complete overhaul of everything. This would create anxiety, pain, fear, and the challenge to identity. The human system is always seeking stability and balance during change. If I seek to impose my values, views, or timing onto the system, I am doing my work and the system is not doing its work. I view myself as a facilitator (which requires great patience) rather than an initiator of change. I always carry the notion that "This is not my organization. I don't own it. It is not my job to make them into what I think they should be. It is my job to help them better decide what they should be."

Be open and appropriately flexible: Planned change is a misnomer. We can't be black and white. Plans to get together are one thing. Change that is close to the core cannot be planned or rushed. I think of change as a flow. Everything is always in process, which requires a high level of intuition, tolerance for ambiguity, and ability to deal with chaos. T-groups have no agenda, but they do make progress. I can always make assumptions about the future based on what I know about the past. But some condition will occur that is beyond my prediction and the future will be different than I imagined.

Meg Wheatley

Bob, these principles are such an important part of the way you have always approached change. It relates to the point you've made about the importance of personal work in OD. We must be the change that we want to see, and there's no way of getting around it.

I was recently given a quote from Parker Palmer, who is a leading light in education. He said, "We teach who we are." It's the same as Gandhi saying, "My life is my message." There's no other testament. It's very powerful.

But let's be careful about time. Change takes time, but civilizations disappear over time. I just read an analogy that helps explain emergence. If a pond is being taken over by lily pads, which can have an exponential growth rate, on day twenty-nine only half of the pond is covered. Three days earlier, on day twenty-six, only a tenth of the pond was covered. It's hard to say, "Watch out." It's hard for us to imagine exponential growth.

The way life evolves and the way you get increased complexity is that you have many local actions. So somebody does something in one department, somebody does something else in another department, somebody does something else in a far-flung division. The same thing happens when a local community changes itself, and then another local community, and then another. They don't stay in isolation; and when they hook up, what you get is emergence.

In science, this is a synonym for self-organization, but I like to separate them a little bit. What you get from connecting local change is a whole new system that emerges. Whatever emerges will be different. It won't just be more than the sum of the parts, it will be different than the parts; it will have a different character, a different flavor to it. And it will exert disproportionate power back down to the local units that created it.

One of the great troubling truths about emergence is that you can't see it till it's happened, actually can't see it coming. So it's not just about not planning a step. Until these local actions hook up, you really don't know what the result will be. That's why globalization happens—a lot of companies doing things independently, for their own reasons, eventually get networked together. And something emerges that exerts a lot of power.

We have power too, however. Once we notice what's emerged, and we notice its highly negative impacts in different parts of the planet; then we have a choice to move from feeling "There's nothing I can do; it's too big" to really stepping forward.

Bob Tannenbaum

It seems to me that values are central to everything you and I have been saying, the foundation of how we do what we do. Values are the constant of what it means to be human. We are talking now of the ways we do our work, the models, methods, and processes. There is one piece that still puzzles me—a lot of what you've written communicates the importance of trusting the process, trusting the unfolding of the meaning. Is that consistent with the other things we've been saying about identity, purpose, and principles?

Meg Wheatley

Absolutely. The process that I trust in absolutely is self-organization. But self-organization doesn't just happen. It is organizing that occurs around an identity. It is a self that gets organized. Which values we choose will predict the form and content of the organizing and the organization itself.

The paradigm shift is at the larger cultural concept of what an organization is. Until lately, the construct was that an organization is a mechanical thing. We didn't have the paradigm that an organization was something that knew how to organize itself. I feel that within the field of OD this new paradigm has been present for a long time, but in terms of the larger culture, it is just beginning.

Bob Tannenbaum

So human beings, in the context of change, can affect the unfolding self-organizing processes?

Meg Wheatley

They can use it by choosing the values and the identity that they organize around. That's the part of this that people find is hardest to understand. We see something like globalization or a school or organization that's not working, and what we're seeing is the artifacts of a whole series of activities that were created because people were organizing around a certain set of values.

Nazi Germany is actually a terrifying example of a self-organized, emergent phenomenon. It didn't start from a master plan. But it organized consistently around certain values that were inherently destructive. And corporations do the same thing. Whatever they say their values are, too often the key values are, "Do anything for profitability, don't make the boss look bad, and protect yourself." And so if you're organizing around those sets of values, then you're going to have an organization that has deep immorality, that has no regard for people really or any other values, even though the nice values are up on the wall.

The way I use organizing as a change theory is that everything that organizes, that comes in the form—a process, a structure, technique, a report, my behavior over time—all those things are a result of having chosen to do what I did because of certain values. I like to use the behavior as the artifact, and say, "Now what was the belief or the value that led to that?"

Self-organization has two words in it, and both describe a process that we can trust. We can trust that everything that comes into form is a result of decisions, of choices. And those choices are influenced dramatically by our beliefs or our values. If you want to change an organization and an individual, then you have to uncover those core beliefs and values and expose them, bring them to the light of day. And then you choose new values, new processes, new relationships based on those values.

Ann Bares

I have been thinking about what models and tools make a difference in my work. The Parker Palmer quote mentioned by Meg, "We teach who we are," says it very well for me. My work with organizations (both the successes and the failures) has taught me to rely on my "inner compass" to guide my efforts rather than any prescribed model or tool. Blind allegiance to models, while ignoring the inner voice that speaks to me, has led me astray on too many occasions.

Models and tools are both helpful and necessary, particularly to provide guidance in areas where one is inexperienced or unsure. I think of them (and here's the mom in me coming out) as a pair of training wheels that keep you on the right path while your own instincts and confidence mature. Eventually, you become comfortable going on your own.

Bill Harris

I've found Chris Argyris' action science to be one of the most powerful tools I've seen. He has observed that, despite what we may claim, most of us usually act as if driven by four internal rules:

- Win instead of lose;
- Define winning the way we want;
- Be rational; and
- Don't be negative.

He claims there is a more productive set of rules we could use in groups:

- Make decisions based on valid and tested data;

- Make group decisions freely and openly; and

- Be committed to ensuring our group follows these rules.

Many introductions to Argyris' work seem to imply it's an incremental approach that anyone can do to make things better. To the contrary, I've found it to be one of the most profoundly difficult tasks and yet one of the most revolutionary and rewarding approaches I've used.

If this is such a difficult transition to make, how does one get started? For me, the key was understanding Argyris' injunction that you can't coerce people into using the more productive rules. As a manager, I felt he was right, but I couldn't understand where that left me. When I finally caught on that it was both ethically wrong and pragmatically impossible to coerce people into this way of working, I began to see breakthroughs in group performance. (I described that project in "Emphasis on Business, Technology, and People Cuts Turnaround Time at Hewlett-Packard's Lake Stevens Division," *National Productivity Review,* Winter, 1998–1999.)

Action learning and research describe an iterative approach that alternates learning (research) and doing (action). They underpin whatever I do. Indeed, action research is the approach from which organization development sprang. I've applied action learning in group settings (for example, project retrospectives) and in individual settings (for example, learning logs).

I find I'm applying all of these tools more and more online rather than in face-to-face work to get better and faster results, as well as saving the cost of travel.

W. Warner Burke

Two comments about method. (The model question is already settled for me. It is, of course, the Burke-Litwin model!)

First, in an assessment of seven successful organizational change efforts (*Best Practices in OD and Change,* 2001) I found that (a) a variety of methods and interventions had been used, and (b) the only thing I could find that all seven had in common was they all had relied on multiple methods and interventions. In other words, no singular intervention did the job. Lesson: Never assume that one intervention or method will bring about organization change.

Second, there is often an initial temptation to start with the organization chart and see what boxes need to be moved around or changed. Sometimes I serve as a traditional management consultant, not always as an OD practitioner. On one such occasion I was asked by a division general manager in a global pharmaceutical firm to take a look at the structure, the organization design of his division. He was experiencing a customer service problem and believed that it could be attributed to a design flaw.

He was assuming a design flaw as the cause, yet the presenting problem was poor customer service. So instead of considering the organization chart initially, I started with the customer and traced the chain of events or activities back into the organization. The result was a recommendation on my part to eliminate a layer of management and to empower frontline service people to act more directly and quickly on behalf of the customer.

I guess this all sounds obvious, but for me there was significant learning. Lesson: Start with the end in mind and "work backwards." And it's hard to go wrong when you begin with the customer.

Nancy Polend

I practice OD from multiple theory bases, as most folks do, and as the complexity of the workplace environment requires. The four theoretical constructs that most influence my work are

1. *Likert's Profile of Organizational Characteristics:* Useful and concrete, Likert's series of fifty-one diagnostic items identifies specific, observable characteristics in several key areas, most notably in the areas of communication, goal setting, degree of teamwork, employee motivation, and employee attitudes. Therefore, it is possible to use the results of his work as a diagnostic and "destination" model for organizations (*The Human Organization,* 1967).

2. *System Theories:* Bob Tannenbaum is so right to call systems orientation foundational. There are many systems theories: boundaries and parts; inputs, throughputs, and outputs; entrophy and equifinality; integration and differentiation; requisite variety; the components of life, therefore, the components of organizations. I use system theories in both general and specific ways in my OD practice, generally, as an overarching way to understand societal, organizational, and individual behavior, dynamics, and evolution. I use specific concepts within them as ways to understand the dynamics within organizations.

3. *Action Research:* As Bob said at the beginning of this conversation, responsibility belongs with the client. Action research puts ownership where it

belongs, in the organization and not with the consultant. It is both a theoretical model and a process for problem solving and change. It describes a scientific way of infusing change into the system by first collecting data, making the data known, doing something different based on the data, and then evaluating the results of the change. Most published depictions of the action research process show it as:

- Perception of the problem or issue;
- Consultation with change agent or consultant;
- Data gathering and initial diagnosis;
- Feedback to key client or client group;
- Joint action planning; and
- Evaluation and new cycle of action research based on results of evaluation.

For me, there is another step before data gathering, which is communication with the stakeholders *before* the process begins on what is *about to happen*, why, and potential pitfalls that may occur. So after "consultation with change agent or consultant," I add the following step:

- Communication with stakeholder group prior to data gathering.

4. *Bolman and Deal's Organizational "Frames":* Bolman and Deal, in *Modern Approaches to Understanding and Managing Organizations* (1984) and *Reframing Organizations* (1997), provide four frames with which to view organizations—the rational frame, the human resource frame, the political frame, and the symbolic frame. These frames describe the various ways organizations operate, the various possible orientations of organizational consultants, and the various categories of possible interventions.

Each of the frames describe both the "biases" of certain organizations, consultants, and interventions, as well as describing separate components of each of these categories. For example, an organization or consultant may operate by default from a rational frame bias—focusing on structure—but will also exhibit humanistic, symbolic, and political components of behavior. Interventions may be focused on one frame and contain components of the others, and so on. Below I have summarized the frames as I interpret them.

Symbolic (views events as secondary in importance to the *meaning* of the events; interventions geared toward the symbolic frame are future search, open space technology, and anything using simulations)
 	
    Key words: rituals, fluid and complex, symbols, metaphors, holistic, values
	Political (organization as an arena for competing for scarce resources; strategic firing, hostile takeovers, sudden reorganizations are political frame interventions)
	
	    Key words: power, coalitions, competition, win/lose, personal influence, charisma

Human Resource (human side of organizations; interventions such as empowerment and participative management programs, job enrichment, appreciative inquiry, and team building)
 	
    Key words: participation, empowerment, enrichment, feelings, democracy, diversity
	Rational (more mechanical aspects of the organization; interventions such as reorganization, job design, and designing work processes)
	
	    Key words: structure, processes, technology, research, experts, resources

Knowing that all of these constructs are present in every organization and paying attention to all of them (as a system) is important because effective interventions include aspects from each of the frames. Like many of my OD colleagues, my bias was in the humanistic frame and I tended to work from this unilateral perspective. Although I didn't know it in the language of Bolman and Deal's frames at the time, I soon found out that introducing a humanistic intervention into a political situation was doomed to fail.

Mike Jay

In my view, change should not be designed; instead, results should be designed, and then change can serve that. Several years ago I heard David Whyte tell a story about one of his consulting assignments. He said, "No one has to change, but everyone has to have the conversation . . . change comes from that."

On the horizon is an additional methodology called SDi, Spiral Dynamics Integral, a collaborative effort between Dr. Don Beck, Ken Wilbur, and many others, who are beginning to move toward dealing with complexity. Spiral Dynamics Integral is based on the work done by Don Beck and Chris Cowan, co-authors of *Spiral Dynamics* (1996).

Briefly, Spiral Dynamics is a way of understanding vertical and horizontal developmental complexity in systems. It helps us realize that not only are people different, but they have a right to be themselves. The premise of SDi is based on the long-time research of Dr. Clare W. Graves, who spent years researching how we create specific types of coping systems to deal with "spiraling" life conditions. The success of this "match" between coping system and life conditions actually produces the need for more sophisticated coping systems in response to the problems created through the success and failure of coping. This continuously oscillating bio-psychosocial-economic change model has become a way to understand complex adaptive systems.

John Agno

Mike, I'm a reader of Spiral Dynamics literature too, and appreciate the difficulty in describing it briefly. It's worth the study, though, to understand it.

One of the key rules of thumb for "spiral leaders" is the importance of taking the pulse of followers through interactive conversations. If the critical mass of thinking within followers is more complex on the spiral than proposed leadership, that leadership can only take control through intimidation or force. Once that leadership grasps power, the more complex thinkers will go into hiding, exile, or premature graves—revolution will certainly be on the horizon.

However, if the leadership model is too far ahead on the spiral, it will destabilize and overwhelm the group or leave them asking, "Where's this idiot coming from? Does anybody know what he/she's talking about?" Many leaders have been drummed out of the corps or banished into oblivion when their thinking became too complex for the followers to understand.

As I coach executives and business owners in developing leadership skills, I am amazed at the lack of clear leadership practice models. What works for me is this: Leadership can be described as a model consisting of a series of interactive conversations that pull people toward becoming comfortable with the language of personal responsibility and commitment.

I believe an effective leader:

- Develops his or her social capital by becoming skilled at managing personal relationships;

- Recognizes that there is an "invisible" structure of personal and business networks that define true influences and interdependencies—and he or she knows how to access and leverage those resources;

- Is strategic in the way he or she shares knowledge, using that knowledge to earn trust and build his or her reputation within the company and industry; and

- Coaches well, using respectful interactive conversations.

Personal transformation happens by asking the right questions—not by providing answers. When you focus on the solution, you are trying to sell the person something. When you allow people to answer their own questions, they discover what they were not aware of—and what is needed to move forward. Personal transformation leads corporate transformation—one person at a time.

Bill Gellermann

John's mention of respectful conversations gives me the opportunity to call attention to a method that is not a method, but rather a way of being. I refer to "dialogue." The word means "meaning flowing through" (dia = flowing thru + logos = meaning). People who have explored the concept and the experience of dialogue have identified its purpose as being "mutual understanding." When I am in dialogue I feel differently than in most other conversation. I think that is because I feel free of fear of criticism or judgment or other people trying to prove that I (or my views) are "wrong," so I can focus my attention on expressing myself/my truth/my view. Of equal importance, my attention is also on truly understanding others' views—and I find that when I do that, they feel the same kind of freedom I feel when I am expressing myself.

For me, dialogue-as-method is a paradox. Dialogue is not a method and, simultaneously, I experience its presence as something like an "ultimate method." It happens when we stop trying to make it happen and simply let the meaning flow.

Matt Minahan

Building on what Bill has just said . . . the practice of "dialogue" was developed (or perhaps invented) by the physicist David Bohm, who believed (or discovered) that there is a "field" that connects all physical matter, and that there is a likely analogue for human beings. He called it the Implicate Order.

He saw the Implicate Order as the field between all human beings that unifies us and makes us all one in the human family. He believed that our own impulses and drives were constantly in tension with this Implicate Order and that we needed a unique practice to still our thinking and impulsive minds in order to allow the Implicate Order to flow through us and have voice.

Dialogue is, as Bill said, a way of being. But it is also a specific practice that has guidelines and rituals that make it difficult to practice in everyday life, especially without the knowledge or consent of a partner. Specifically, the practice of dialogue suggests that the pace of conversation be greatly slowed down from our normal talk. There should be a noticeable pause between the end of one person's comments and the beginning of the next person's comments.

While all of these things happen in a split second in our normal conversation, Bohm believed that, when we slowed them down and paid attention to them one at a time, we could set aside our impulsive and selfish selves and make a more thoughtful contribution to the greater whole via dialogue . . . thus giving voice to the Implicate Order that exists between and among us all.

I'm in a learning group, and we make sure to practice dialogue at least once every time we convene. We find that the results are powerful and quite different from the conversation that we have in the normal course of our learning and work together.

Paula Griffin

We've been speaking of conversation and the skills that make conversation an effective consulting or coaching method. One of those skills is asking questions, I'm sure you agree. A good bit of our training in OD is about giving us frameworks to ask the right questions. To some extent, that's what the models we love do—they prompt us to ask the questions that matter.

Bruce Mabee

I believe that the "right" questions are among the core interventions and that finding the right question at any moment is an immense challenge. A wise-looking delivery of a "wrong" question is at least as damaging as a powerful, "wrong," expert answer.

I do take the risks of raising potent questions. The main hope is that the question will connect individual perceptions to systemic stuff. One risk is that questions can go "wrong" and create so much confusion that the clients' motivation evaporates. Questions can also bring harm at times by creating too much clarity (oversimplification) that results in the clients quitting their struggles.

When someone asks, "What are some really good questions?" I have few answers; it's all so situational. However, there are some questions that I happen to love and probably overuse. One question is a good threat to my image as a consultant: "How often do I check to see if my 'really good questions' fit the theory I espouse?"

Another pet question of mine is the "last question" in a sequence: "What *should* I have asked you?" This, of course, often begins a deeper dialogue, rather than ending the discussion!

I am sharing these observations about questions as a "core" method, and examples of pet questions, hoping to trigger others' reactions about how we practitioners foist both useful and counterproductive methods onto our clients. I find it important to remember the mix of good and harm that any choice of intervention inevitably achieves. Is anyone else interested in this duality?

Paula Griffin

There was an incident that happened during my graduate work. Bill Dyer was there to lecture on small-group interventions—team building. We sat with pencils raised—the guy who wrote the book on team building would tell us which instrument or survey to use. Our careers would be assured. And then he said, "I don't use surveys or instruments anymore. I've found that I can get everything I need with just a few questions."

"What??" our shocked expressions said. "What do I write here in my notebook?" Naturally, we asked him, "Which questions?" and raised our pencils again. He said "It depends."

Eventually, he did share with us two favorite questions he said he had asked many times:

1. "How did things get to be the way they are around here?" (Interesting question.)

2. "What happens when you tell management the bad news?" (We all knew the answer for most of our organizations, of course. Tell management bad news? I don't think so.)

Two more questions I like include one from a consultant/coach who seemed to have just one question: "What's up?" It seemed to get things started for him every time.

And the second is from Jim Lukaszewski, a crisis communications consultant, who asks one question repeatedly: "What has changed since last we talked?" He says it often uncovers critical information. I'd love to hear other peoples' favorite questions. What are yours?

Marti Kaplan

Well, Paula . . . it depends. When I'm going in cold, with no background information at all, I used to use:

1. What's good around here?
2. What's bad around here?
3. What helps you get your work done?
4. What gets in your way?

I can't remember right now who to attribute that to—I haven't used it in a long time. The last time I did, I interviewed seven people and got ninety pages of notes (I'm an almost-vertabim note taker). Now I do a few preliminary interviews to find out the questions I want to ask. And at the end of each interview, I ask, "What other questions should I be asking?"

Matt Minahan

Mine are similar, Marti. Depending on the context and the issues to be worked on, I typically ask some version of the following. They normally get me all I need.

1. What works well here, and why do you think so?
2. What could work better here, and what do you recommend?
3. What do people talk about here at meetings and in the hallways?
4. Do you like it here? Well enough to stay?
5. What else should I be asking about?

Robert McCarthy

My questions have changed over twenty-two years in private practice. Early on I asked questions from a checklist that was my distillation of what I thought described a healthy organization. Later I asked questions intended to determine strengths and weaknesses so that I might solve most problems that impeded effectiveness. Today, in a conversation with an organization leader, I am interested in three things: the situation now, the vision for what is possible, and whether I am moved by this vision. These aren't really questions. They are more the focus of a conversation that is reflected back and leads to a second conversation and a plan of first steps.

As we talk over the plan and decide on our goals I am interested in learning:

1. What is working now (the assets and resources we have to draw on)?

2. Where are the "land mines"?

3. Who must be involved and what are the most effective methods we might use to involve them (for example, large groups, interviews, teleconferences, and so forth)?

The rest evolves.

Bill Harris

I'm delighted with all the wisdom here. Regarding questions, I'm indebted to Bob Dick of Southern Cross University for "Hmm." Actually, I don't recall his exact question, but he encourages the use of such a statement to keep people talking without leading the conversation.

I'm not 100 percent sure where I got this, but I've also been known to ask, "If you could wave a magic wand, what would you do for this organization?"

Paula Griffin

I've long thought that you could ask almost any question, including "How 'bout them Cards?" and people would tell you what's on their minds. That may be true to an extent, but the questions you all have posed would be likely to get to the issues sooner.

We started "back when" talking about models of change. I worked with a man who often said, "All models are wrong; some are useful." To me, models are useful if they make complex things understandable or help us organize large quantities of information. Do any of you have a model you think is really powerful for right now?

One model I love for our work is one I have titled "The Change Equation." I did not invent the Change Equation. It has a strong provenance—it started with David Gleicher and was promoted by Dick Beckhard and Reuben Harris in their book, *Organizational Transitions.* It really took off when Kathie Dannemiller renamed the elements so they became easy to understand and remember. All I did was paste on a title, which gave me the ability to use it in articles and speeches.

Most people understand it quickly, so it's especially useful for presenting to clients. It adds concreteness to discussions of the elements of change and sometimes provides a vocabulary with which to discuss those elements.

Here's how it reads: C = DVF > R. Simple, but surprisingly comprehensive. In English, that might read: *Change* will happen when, and to the extent to which, *Dissatisfaction* with the current state, times a clear *Vision* of the desired future state, times a concrete understanding of the *First steps* to get there, is greater than the *Resistance* or cost. The core of the equation is multiplicative. The foundation of change, or at least the first key element, is dissatisfaction, which creates energy for the change. People generally won't spend time, energy, and money to solve a non-problem.

But each of the elements is required. While clear visions of a lovely future (V) or great training, equipment, and resources (all elements of F) will not generally overcome a lack of the energy supplied by dissatisfaction, a small amount of dissatisfaction can still lead to great change if there is a compelling vision with enough resources to make it possible, and the energy of a core committed group.

The Change Equation isn't the only model for change that I like, but it has helped me help folks do some solid strategizing. For that I often thank David, Dick, Reuben, and Kathie.

Robert (Jake) Jacobs

I too have found this "change equation" to be a helpful way for people to understand the elements required for change to occur—it's clear and readily applicable.

However, over time in my work, I found that the equation was a great predictor for change to occur, but wasn't enough to sustain changes made over time. For that to occur, there needed to be another element: the capacities or competencies required to sustain these changes. These capacities or competencies could take the form of mindsets, processes, systems, structures, skills, knowledge, or anything that supported people in creating sustainable change.

Amended to include this new element, the equation then reads: C = DVCF > R.

Without adding this element of *capacity* or *competence* into the equation, you run the risk of creating "teflon" change that could leave you in a worse situation than if you had never attempted to improve things in the first place because of people's hopes being dashed and their "proof" that things will never change being reinforced.

In general, though, I don't think I have any "favorite models." I think the best models aren't the ones *I* like the best, but are the ones that are most helpful to the people in an organization in getting where they want to go and becoming how they want to be.

The broader my potential pool of methods and models, the more I can offer to spark our collective creativity. Sometimes I fear that what we like can take precedence over what makes sense for our clients.

John Adams

I guess a good many of us use this or similar formulae. I changed the Beckhard and Harris formula for change by adding two more qualities, so for me it reads C = f(B,D,V,F,O)>R (C = Change; B = Belief that the change is both possible and desirable; D = Disruption of status quo (a la Lewin); V = understood and accepted Vision/Goals; F = First steps; O = role of Others [everyone around the boundary] can ensure success—either by getting "in" or by staying "out"; and R = Resistance [or investment in the status quo]).

Regarding change I once spent an entire week of Open Space at one of the annual Organizational Transformation conferences asking people to tell me success stories from times when they had successfully made and sustained deep pattern changes in their lives. When I explored the stories I had collected, I found a limited number of widely shared qualities. Nearly everyone had some version of:

1. Incredible level of commitment;
2. Clear picture of the outcome;
3. A next step to take (no one mentioned plan);
4. Some kind of mechanism or structure that required repetitions of the new pattern;
5. Unconditional support; and
6. Patience—trust the process, trust spirit, and so on.

When I later asked for stories of successful shared pattern change (culture change) at work, I found many the same qualities. The commitment issue (number 1 above) included consistent, persistent, vocal, and visible articulation of this commitment by all sponsors and stakeholders.

One of the "mechanisms for requiring repetitions of the new" was the establishment of clear accountabilities. Whenever I see a large-scale change effort fall apart, I find that many of the essential qualities I found from my story gathering are missing.

Robert McCarthy

You asked about particularly powerful change models. I have been using one that, with the right leaders, is very powerful. It has three basic elements:

1. "What is now"—an acknowledgment of the present. You can use any form of assessment that results in a substantial number of key folks saying, "Yes, that's the way it is around here now." Regardless of the method to produce the data, the data needs to be "warm." That is, it needs to have enough emotional content to produce energy.

2. A leader's vision of the future that is compelling and, through dialogue, results in hope and the desire to see it come to pass. This may require several iterations and some refinement using all forms of communication: electronic, face-to-face, and so on.

3. Once folks are interested and become committed to what can be, then a series of practical actions led by key folks (execs, managers, supervisors, staff) to move in the desired direction. This, coupled with communication of steps underway, successes, and the like, demonstrates that "this is for real" and not just words.

In summary, assessing strengths and weaknesses to work the problems is not enough. An appreciative inquiry-like approach where the focus is on what works and a vision for the future does. Further, the three elements can and are incorporated in many of our change processes. For example, large-group work incorporates these elements in a particular form, is powerful, and works wonderfully well to unfreeze and move a system. The particular change method is less important than the three elements.

I have used this three-step model to create a labor-management alliance in a utility company and to redesign a large community justice system and am currently using it in the redesign of a university nursing school and a county health department. Each of these settings is complex, bureaucratic, and resistant to change. In each of these cases, and several others, there were/are solid senior leaders, without whom the model does not work.

My conclusion is that if there is sufficient tension between what is and what can be, coupled with a series of actions driven by those affected, quite rapid constructive change occurs.

Glenda Eoyang

All this talk of models reminds me that we are prone to "model wars," searching for the one that is best of them all. Human systems dynamics helps us think about high dimensional systems in which there are multiple definitions of "good." From this perspective, the "best" approach is the one that fits—with the practitioner's skills, the client's budget and schedule, the group's history, the organization's environment, the presenting problem or opportunity, and a variety of other determining dimensions that affect the complex dynamics of the human system under investigation.

As professionals, our job is to be proficient in as many methods as possible, to collaborate with others who are proficient where we are not, to know the strengths and weaknesses of each approach, and to work with the client to select the intervention that is most likely to improve the dynamics of system. "Most likely" is the best we can do because complex dynamics are neither controllable nor predictable.

From traditional perspectives, we assumed that we should be able to know enough about the system and about the mechanics of our interventions to predict outcomes of our actions. We should be able to promise outcomes to our clients with money-back guarantees. If we couldn't produce the promised outcomes, we blamed ourselves (not enough data collection, insufficient skills), the method (too time-consuming or not comprehensive enough), or the client (resistant to change, conflict averse). In contrast, complex dynamics are inherently unpredictable. A very small difference in the initial conditions can generate tremendous differences in the end state of the system. You cannot know enough to predict how the process will play out. The system is always smarter and more creative than any observer. This perspective frees us from the delusion of control and opens opportunities to work with and within the system to optimize opportunities as they emerge.

In these and many other ways, moving from the mindset of development to one of dynamics allows us to transcend the questions that we have dwelt in unproductively for so long. Human systems dynamics honors the learnings of the past and establishes a framework for the next generation of learning in our field of study and practice.

David Jamieson

Models organize phenomena. Theory helps us to understand. Both are imperfect in human affairs, so they are very helpful and never enough! I used to think you could study hard enough to know all you needed. Now I know you cannot. Something always comes along that doesn't fit well. How you learn to deal with these and approach such situations is what mastery is really about. Experience builds "frames" or models for us—a way of thinking and sense-making. But experience also frees you from having to use them!

By their very nature, models are linear simplifications of nonlinear, complex phenomena, especially in the arena of human behavior and organizational dynamics. So there are always more variables, forces, and interactions occurring to produce more phenomena than any model will explain.

For example, my favorite model is my *alignment model*, which was developed over many years, primarily from practice, but also influenced by my knowledge of theory and similar models. Basically, it portrays the interdependence among five organizational components (strategy, structure, culture, systems, and behavior) and has been useful to me in diagnosis, intervention strategy, and education.

While it is a systems model, it certainly doesn't include all the variables that make up the organizational system. One of the primary theses in the model is that strategy should drive design (structure, culture, and systems), which in turn drives behavior. But we also know that sometimes that sequence can happen in reverse, or that personality and motivation can intervene to produce unexpected behavior, or that pockets in the organization can operate counter-culturally and completely outside of the structure and systems! Yet at a macro level, the model has helped us to understand existing problems and bring components into better alignment and consequently better performance.

I think the way to use models *and* move beyond them is to first educate yourself in your primary areas of interest (for example, the five components of the alignment model) and then to pay attention to what deviates from or can't be explained by the areas you know something about and their assumed relationships. What deviates or can't be explained are then the areas to learn more about—to further inquire in pursuit of explaining more. So the more we can understand and explain, the more we can feel comfortable about our model(s)-in-use and the more we know our path of inquiry is going in the right direction!

Bruce Mabee

Any time I've taken a half-hour to list models and tools that I use frequently, several dozen jump out. Then I improvise and combine these with other models and tools—and try to make the result as organic, conversational, and "non-tool-like" as possible. I hope it ends up simpler for the client, but the path to simplicity is not simple!

I'm showing my "short list," hoping others will share their short lists. What do you use weekly or monthly? I'm also curious—how do you choose and mix and match the tools as a project progresses?

Here is my current short list—models and tools that enter my work every week or so. I've named the authors I know, the field in which I first used it (if not OD), and key words about elements that stand out to me.

- *Process Consulting*: Edgar Schein. Feed back observations in real time to illuminate system.

- *Force Field Analysis:* Kurt Lewin. Brainstorm broadly: What helps and gets in the way of this goal?

- *Situation-Target-Plan:* When one element of a system changes, other elements change.

- *Open Systems Planning:* Dick Beckhard. Map the demands of each stakeholder.

- *Getting to Yes:* Roger Fischer/William Ury. Negotiation. Drive hard for the common goals.

- *System Design Process:* J.C. Jones. Find truly broad options, then design.

- *Strategy Switching:* J. C. Jones. Regularly compare spontaneous thoughts to strategy.

- *Design by Doing:* Robert Fathergill. Drawing (Art). Actual affect versus "what should work."

- *Information Funnel:* Journalism. Headline, lead paragraph, details, in descending importance.

- *Tai Chi Principle:* Al Huang. Our daily life is literally a dance, if we take a second to notice.

I frequently need models and tools that I do not find in any "toolkits" or lists of interventions. When this happens, I develop tools to fit. Here are three that I've developed and continued using for years:

The Four Postures of Influence: "Postures" are how we treat people. Consciously or not, every action toward others carries an attitude, a style, a spin, an angle. There are four fundamental postures: *to* them, *for* them, *with* them, or *by* them. In any attempt to influence others, the posture determines how they react as much as the substance. Thus, managing postures is a core ingredient in leadership, coaching, and consulting.

Unlike specific techniques of communication or leadership, we do not train people how to "do" postures, but rather how to manage the postures they already use. Seeing these *meta* behaviors in action, recognizing how people are responding to our habitual postures, is usually a wake-up call ("The Four Postures of Influence," *Training Today,* July/August, 2000).

The Powers of Three: "What can we *usefully* do in this current business predicament?" Three dimensions provide a template to quickly grasp a complex situation—*scope, depth,* and *change.* This leadership framework offers "safe habits" of systemic diagnosis to avoid getting lost in the trees of long, elaborate assessments. These "powers" enable powerful people to keep their head on straight under pressure.

Each power is a simple concept, easy to do. The goal is to mentally "sketch" any situation—and quickly change the sketch as reality changes. The key is to practice each power until it becomes a habit, then add another power until two powers, then three, become habitual even under stress.

- Scope, the first power, acknowledges that any presenting problem links to a larger strategic context and to the immediate moment. The "Three Rings" is a visual tool to help us to keep conscious of the "scope"—and gives a language for discussing scope issues with clients and stakeholders.

- Depth, the second power, links "hard stuff" (technical logistics), "soft stuff" (relationships), and "inner stuff" (values). A tornado graphically illustrates how forces intertwine.

- Change deals with timeframes. It illustrates how our work, in short "loops" of time, influences major change in long loops of time. "Change" ties together the other two powers ("The Powers of Three: Practical Business Diagnosis Whether or Not They Ask," *Training Today,* September/October, 2000).

Quick Loops/Rapid Evolution: "Quick looping" is a simple idea for using time differently. Also known as rapid action cycles, this compressed method of action research bypasses the normal planning/problem-solving steps. Instead of a linear sequence, like "gather data, analyze, create alternatives, plan, implement, evaluate. . .," quick looping *drives toward the reality test.* The mission is adaptive learning in a harsh reality—assuming that the world won't stop while we analyze and plan what to do next ("Two Paths Under Pressure: Lack of Time or Loops of Time?" *Training Today*, November/December, 2000).

So the tools I use tend to be the extremely adaptable, open-ended ones, which directly get to the stakeholder viewpoints and then shift gears quickly as views shift.

Glenn Allen-Meyer

As we name our favorite models, I'd like to mention one of the success killers for all change programs—their names. Give a change program a name and listen to how quickly people marginalize it with clever permutations of the name and statements of "another flavor of the month." I passionately believe that we in this field need to recognize that a great deal of resistance to change in today's organizations simply comes from the fact that people have had nearly thirty years of "change in a box." All it takes to trigger cynicism today is a well-named change program.

So my favorite model for the implementation of organizational change is something I call the "nameless change" model. It's called "nameless" because of my experience over the years with people's reactions to traditional models of change that:

- Define the scope/mission/et cetera (with or without participatory processes);
- Give the change a "name" that is announced and hyped throughout the organization; and
- Market change "programs" like commodities for people's "buy-in."

People feel the same way about change as they feel about the uninvited SPAM emails that clog their inboxes. To be successful in this climate, a change should be a negotiated settlement between the interests of the people calling for the change and the ongoing work demands of the understaffed and information-drenched people who must implement it. It should be positioned as a potential added value to the real-time work being done without doing a "sales job" on people. In my experience, people resist the hype more than they do the potential merits. With this nameless approach, cynicism does not have the necessary stimulus for taking root.

Patty Sadallah

I love models. I have dozens of them hidden in the recesses of my mind, ready to jump out to help me think through a situation or a problem. The models that I choose to store away have a few things in common:

- They have "ah ha" validity. That is, they are simple enough to be validated by everyday experience so that when they are explained, the person can honestly say, "Ah ha!"

- They pass the airplane test. This is about simplicity again. They are free enough of our OD jargon that they can be explained in just a few minutes on an airplane to a complete "non-OD" stranger. When this is done well, you can see understanding rather than a glazed look on their faces.

- They help you think. If a model doesn't help you think through a problem or a challenge in a new and different way, it's not worth the napkin on which it was scratched.

- It can be passed on to the client. I always make it a point to teach models to my clients in order to empower them to think more clearly.

Here is a short list of some of my favorites:

1. *The compass model* for organizational dynamics (Richard Haass, *The Power to Persuade*). It's very simple. Place your clients in the center of the compass, your boss at north, your subordinates at south, internal colleagues over whom you have no formal authority at east, and people outside the organization with whom you must partner at west. The model advises of the ways you must interact with each of these groups, who to speak well of, when, and to whom, and the rules for communication to build relationships and maintain trust. Some behaviors, like "contributing to a favor bank" work for all of the audiences. Some are more audience-specific, good political skills like "never bad mouth the boss or a competitor in public."

2. *The Team Performance Model*, by Alan Drexler and David Sibbet. This looks complicated, but is really quite logical. What I like most about the TPM is that it assumes that all people come into the team experience asking the same questions (both personal and task-oriented) in a certain order. If a question is answered in a satisfactory way, we naturally jump to the next question. The model helps to show when the team should be addressing which type of question.

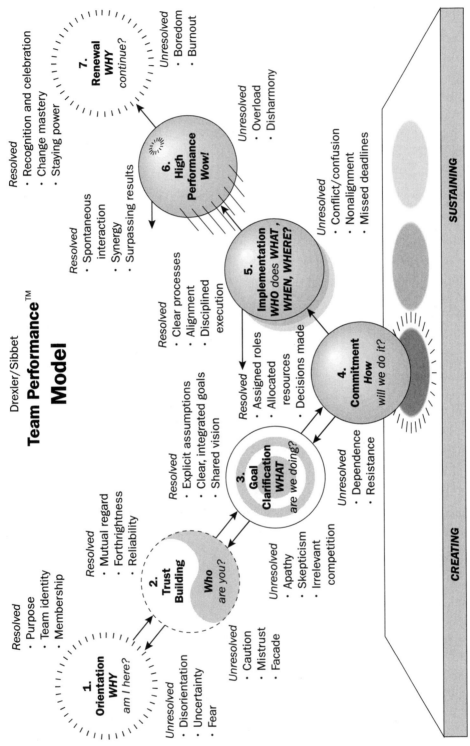

Drexler/Sibbet

Team Performance™

Model

1. Orientation WHY *am I here?*

Resolved
· Purpose
· Team identity
· Membership

Unresolved
· Disorientation
· Uncertainty
· Fear

2. Trust Building *Who are you?*

Resolved
· Mutual regard
· Forthrightness
· Reliability

Unresolved
· Caution
· Mistrust
· Facade

3. Goal Clarification WHAT *are we doing?*

Resolved
· Explicit assumptions
· Clear, integrated goals
· Shared vision

Unresolved
· Apathy
· Skepticism
· Irrelevant competition

4. Commitment *How will we do it?*

Resolved
· Assigned roles
· Allocated resources
· Decisions made

Unresolved
· Dependence
· Resistance

5. Implementation WHO *does* WHAT, WHEN, WHERE?

Resolved
· Clear processes
· Alignment
· Disciplined execution

Unresolved
· Conflict/confusion
· Nonalignment
· Missed deadlines

6. High Performance *Wow!*

Resolved
· Spontaneous interaction
· Synergy
· Surpassing results

Unresolved
· Overload
· Disharmony

7. Renewal WHY *continue?*

Resolved
· Recognition and celebration
· Change mastery
· Staying power

Unresolved
· Boredom
· Burnout

CREATING

SUSTAINING

© 1993-1999 Allan Drexler & David Sibbet. Used with permission.

The model is diagnostic, too. To the right of each stage, the authors show behaviors or symptoms that indicate that the question is being answered properly and the arrows move you to the next stage. To the left, there are behaviors and symptoms that show that a group is stuck at that stage. The arrows on that side go back up to indicate that if a group is stuck at that stage, they need to back up to the previous stage and work on addressing that question. Groups can easily find their behaviors on the model, and then they know right where the group is at that moment and on what stage they need to focus their attention.

3. *Situational Leadership,* by Paul Hersey and Ken Blanchard. This is an oldie but a goody. Situational Leadership respects that different leadership behavior is needed for different employees, at different times, for different tasks. By considering both aptitude (experience/skill) and interest (motivation), the model enables managers to see that it is appropriate to support an experienced person differently for a new task. It's especially helpful for executive coaching because it helps to explain what happens when people have worked up to jobs that they liked and were good at, and something shifts and they find themselves being asked to do work that they don't like and are not good at. They have been managed for years in a hands-off kind of way and don't see themselves needing direct supervision. But for the new tasks, direct supervision is needed. Executive coaches can use this model to help explain the impact of this kind of change in a way that helps people to accept.

All of this fits with one of my long-held theories that *all* change should be introduced as only *10 percent new.* Even if the change feels like it is 110 percent new, people can only adjust to 10 percent of change at a time. A coach or manager may say to the client, "You are still selling the same product; you are still the best in the business; the only thing that's different here is our new computer system, and in that piece of your work we'll need to hold your hand a little bit."

4. *Seeing Systems,* by Barry Oshry. Oshry says that, in any situation, we may be at the top (with our subordinates), middle (with colleagues), or bottom (with our boss or an angry partner). Sometimes (like a staff meeting) we could be all three. It helps people sort through the complexity of relationships and empathize with all three roles because it helps them to see that they can play all three roles. It also helps people become more aware of blind spots. A person cannot see more than one level above them and one level below them.

This means that all of the other levels are blind. This awareness can really help people be more conscientious about communication.

5. *Systems Thinking,* by Peter Senge. This definitely does not pass the simplicity test, but once you understand it, it is very useful. The biggest challenge has been coming up with language that can explain this simply to clients. Systems thinking helps the client look deeper than the symptoms and encourages them to find root causes and primary solutions rather than Band-Aids®.

6. *Strategic Marketing.* Tom Woll and I designed this model to help non-profit organizations learn how to market in tough economic times through listening rather than selling. We first used the model with social workers, training them to go out into the community and listen first to consumers, then to those who funded services, then to be creative about meeting the need, then to listen again.

   It was a challenge for the employees to shift from thinking that they intuitively knew what was needed to actually finding out what needs existed and then devising ways to meet these needs. Specifically, the strategic marketing plan included the following elements:

   • *Identify vital community needs.* This is accomplished by sending people out to interview and listen to a variety of audiences, consumers, funders, potential funders. The trick was to make sure they listened and didn't try to sell anything before they truly heard the messages of these audiences clearly. The focus was to ask the question, "If we could come up with a way to meet this need, would you pay for it?"

   • *Determine ways to meet identified vital needs.* This entailed looking carefully at what was said, not just through the filter of what we do and already are good at, but for what was really needed. Then the task is finding the talent to meet the need. Who could we partner with who could really meet this need?

   • *Negotiate "win/win," creative programs.* Partnering with others who had compatible niches to come up with the most creative and cost-effective services that would meet the need was the challenge of this phase.

   • *Obtain feedback and take corrective action.* Listen again. Are you coming up with what they said they wanted? If not, change it.

Although this model was created specifically for non-profits, I think there is for-profit applicability. In two years, Catholic Charities Services Corporation in Cleveland has created 111 new services in eight counties and developed $8 million in new revenue!

Carol Lyles Shaw

I love this conversation about models. And since I teach an "Intro to OD" course for entering practitioners, I have to refresh myself about models and tools periodically. I *do* have my favorites. I tend to go back to Weisbord's boxes—the original six, plus external environment. I use it for everything—diagnosis, design, during the contracting, feedback, and so on. I may not speak to every box, but I always refer to it as one way of assuring that I am taking a systemic view.

I begin with a clear definition of the client system that I am working with. Is it a department of a large organization, the entire group of paid employees in a company or government agency, or paid employees plus volunteers? Yes, I start by defining the system as the people in it—not the services or products produced. Services/products and then processes are other ways of mapping the system, and it is often interesting to define or map both and then overlay them to see whether they match!

After I've defined the client system, I begin to work through the boxes. These are not in order of importance except that leadership is the foundation.

Box	Description and Conditions
Leadership	I start here, not because I am anti-democratic, but because my experience tells me that appropriate and ethical use of power, legitimate authority, and influence are key to any change. Who are the leaders and what do they care about? What do their past and current actions tell us? What is the level of trust in them by others? How much do they trust each other (peers) and their subordinates? Who are the informal leaders and the power brokers? What are the leaders willing to risk in order to change? What is most important to them to preserve?

Box	Description and Conditions
Purpose	Where are we going and why? How lofty or mundane is our vision? Who knows about it? Who needs to know? What do we actually do for others—product or service?
Rewards	If we get there (to the vision), what will I get? What are the rewards worth to me? What are the consequences/punishments, and do I care about those either? These are the questions on everyone's mind—often unstated (assumed to be known) or undiscussable (taboos, for example, talking about wanting higher salaries and performance bonuses in social service organizations).
Integrating Mechanisms and Supporting Technologies **Weisbord's "Helpful Mechanisms"**	These mechanisms and technologies help people get the work done—when they exist and work well. When the official ones break down, people will always invent ways around them. If they don't exist, people will *always* invent them—and may deny their existence. They may be "covert processes" because they lack official sanction. Examples of integrating mechanisms and supporting technologies include the PC, email, grapevines, approval forms and policies, standard operating procedures, voicemail, other computer systems, Internet, accounting/measurement processes, and socialization processes, such as orientations and training programs. The list is infinite, and we sometimes confuse the mechanisms and technologies for the whole system. These are tools or artifacts of the system. Some of them may be quite elegant; others may be very primitive. *All* tell us something about the people and what it is like to work there.
Relationships	"Who do I know and who knows me? Who do I trust and who trusts me? Who do I care about and who cares about me?" These questions have answers that can change in a heartbeat. Changes in the rewards or structure, for example, will have an impact. Any data collected must always be seen as a snapshot of the *past* and not necessarily a map to the present or the future. Group identities (race, class, gender, and so forth) will also have major impact and must be taken into consideration as well. Relationship factors may be among the organization's "undiscussables."

Box	Description and Conditions
Structure	How are roles and responsibilities defined? Who knows this information? Have critical conflicts been discussed and resolved, or are they covert? Power and authority reside in structure. Lack of structure can kill an organization. Structure may be loose, but it must exist. In the absence of leader-defined structure, people will invent it in ways that meet their needs.
External Environment	The world outside the defined boundaries of the client system. This world might be as large as the earth or as small as a town or the people who work on my floor who are not members of my team. The key is to recognize that all system boundaries are simultaneously rigid and fluid and permeable. Rigidity is an illusion, of course, since all systems are influenced to some degree by everything around them.

For the original, see Marvin Weisbord's *Organizational Diagnosis: Six Places to Look for Trouble with or Without a Theory.*

And, although it is not a change model, I also use Block's Flawless Consulting Model as a way of ensuring that I will have what I need to build an effective collaboration with the client. Our models tend to be "client" focused and flawless-ness makes sure that I don't overlook myself as part of the system. Like others, I also create models and I encourage my students and other entering practitioners to see themselves as discoverers—scholar practitioners who will help build the knowledge of the field.

Nancy Roggen

Carol, thanks for mentioning one of my favorites—Weisbord's Six-Box Model—and your addition of the external world (which I think I added silently and will add explicitly with my next client).

Often when I'm stuck I go back to Dick Beckhard's focus for interventions and check to see if the Goals, Roles, and Processes are commonly understood—and then, and perhaps only then, focus on Interpersonal Relationships. Dick held that until the first three are clarified and agreed on, it does not make sense to plow into the area of great interest for many OD practitioners (and heaven knows I've been there and am often tempted to go back) of interpersonal relationships. No matter how much "relationship work" we do, if there's a disconnect in goals, roles, and processes, the interpersonal relationship symptoms will continue to be present.

I'm also attracted to Appreciative Inquiry as a vehicle that helps people connect with times in their lives when things worked well. I can forget the feelings and ingredients of successful work when I'm in a group or situation that is "not working." Starting with a sense memory of a positive creates a possibility of positive in the current situation and definitely opens the space for dialogue.

Becky DeStefano

I'm delighted that you have listed many of my favorite models and books. I would add a couple:

- *Action Research:* My background as a basketball coach leads me to appreciate the act of getting data, acting on it or reacting to it, and then getting more data, constantly changing the way you actually do something.

- Kathie Dannemiller's group process and whole-scale change models and tools, which counsel getting the whole system in the room.

- Dick and Emily Axelrod's *Terms of Engagement*: The four keys that Dick Axelrod describes for this are widening the circle of involvement, connecting people to each other and to ideas, creating communities for action, and embracing democracy.

- Marvin Weisbord's work taught me to ask two important questions: "What business are we in?" and "Who is the client?"

- Peter Block's ideas on authenticity made a big difference for me and for internal consultants I teach. Internal consultants have often believed their job was to listen and go do. Enter a meeting and authentically react to what you see and hear? Radical.

- Speaking of internals, the change equation discussed earlier is something I've found internal consultants can grasp quickly and can use to guide them in asking the right questions.

- Mintzberg introduced me to the Seven S model (Structure, Strategy, Superordinate goals, Staff, Systems, Style of leadership, Skills), which is so helpful in scanning an organization. It has great impact in teaching systems thinking.

- Senge—I really liked the idea of thinking in terms of action and impact. But for me, the thing I valued most from Senge was the Ladder of Inference. It helps so much to remind us that when we and the client walk into the room, we are both at the top of the ladder. We have observed data and had experiences, selected data, added meaning, made assumptions, drawn conclusions, adopted beliefs, and taken action. So here we are, and our work as a consultant is to walk back down that ladder and understand it.

The thing I notice about our use of models as I read through some of the other comments is that the basics are still standing. It doesn't have to be complicated to be able to help us and our clients understand and guide us through complexity. A deep understanding of the simplest models can create profound impact on an organization.

Gary Rossi

So far no one has mentioned the Criteria for Performance Excellence (also known as the Malcolm Baldrige National Quality Award Criteria) in these discussions. The criteria and model offer categories for reflecting organizational success (results) and ask how the organization approaches and deploys key elements across the other six categories, which include:

- *Organizational Results*—Describes organizational success and achievement in organizational and operational performance measures, specifically customer-focused results, financial and market results, employee care results, and organizational effectiveness results.

- *The Senior Leadership System*—Asks questions like, "How do senior leaders set and deploy organizational values, short-term and longer-term directions, and performance expectations, including a focus on creating and balancing value for customers and other stakeholders?"

- *Strategic Planning and Management*—Considers such topics as, "What is your overall strategic planning process, including key steps, key participants, and your short-term and longer-term planning time horizons?"

- *Customer and Market Focus*—Requires information like, "How do you determine or target customers, customer groups, and/or markets?"

- *Information and Analysis*—Asks, among other things, "How do you select and align measures/indicators for tracking daily operations and overall organizational performance?"

- *Employee Care*—Considers, "How do you organize and manage work and jobs to promote cooperation, initiative/innovation, your organizational culture, and the flexibility to keep current with business needs?"

- *Process Management*—Part of its seventeen areas of inquiry include, "How do you incorporate changing customer/market requirements into product/service designs and production/delivery systems and processes?"

The criteria also emphasize establishing cycles of refinement, improvement, and a self-evaluation process for fostering the development of the learning organization.

A five-year study of more than six hundred quality award winners by two professors, Dr. Vinod Singhal of the Georgia Institute of Technology and Dr. Kevin Hendricks of the College of William and Mary, shows that by using the criteria, the study companies experienced consistent improvement in value of their common stock, operating income, sales, return on sales, employment, and asset growth. Find out more about the Baldrige criteria either at www.nist.gov or www.calexcellence.org.

Jean Neumann

I still rely on basic educational design methodology and basic cycles of organizational development that I learned thirty years ago. There are a few things I think are important though:

- For projects lasting three months to five years, form an internal change agent team.

- Undertake a short data-feedback process in order to be able to genuinely negotiate and plan any subsequent rounds of intervention.

- Craft interventions into iterations (the way most organizations intentionally develop). This requires skill at selecting the initial two rounds of people to be involved in diagnosis and in negotiating interventions.

- Include representatives of differing sides of core strategic debates.

- Tempting as it is, don't allow the client to ask you to decide the nature of an intervention without much of a negotiated planning process with an internal change agent team. Much of the debate about how to proceed reveals cultural and structural issues relevant to the success of subsequent attempts to bring about changes.

Mike Mitchell

As OD practitioners, we often describe ourselves as consultants who work on systems, yet do most of our work with little pieces and parts of systems. Typically, the reason for this is that we are not invited to work on the whole system, or the presenting problem is seen as occurring in only one part of the system, and even if it is just a symptom, the pressure is on working with the place where the symptom occurs. We are rarely system consultants because we don't get the chance or we don't make getting the chance happen.

As I have practiced over the years, I have come to some startling conclusions about organizations. Some will sound cynical, but I hope you'll consider them. Here they are

1. Most managers do not understand how the work gets done in the organization. When asked to draw a process map, the managers will draw one quite different from those drawn by the people actually doing the work.

2. Professional managers (non-owners) will often not have the best interests of the organization as their number-one concern. Instead, the concerns will be power, protection from vulnerability, and siphoning off as many of the organization's funds into the pockets of top management as possible.

3. Fully 70 percent of the work that organizations engage in is likely to have nothing to do with adding value for customers, and is thus nothing more than waste. The real frontier for OD is to help organizations deal with this issue.

4. Being Rogerian is not very effective. If we truly are experts in organization effectiveness, we will have a good idea about what needs to be done. Advocacy, rather than hanging back so that the client feels in control, is a better style. By all means, build the client's skills, but push for the best choices.

5. Having representatives is a poor way to do things. When we redesign a system using selected members of the organization to study the issue and come up with a better approach, the solution may be okay, but it will never be as good as if everyone was involved, and it will never get the buy-in and ongoing commitment if everyone is not involved. Organizations will resist whole-system interventions, claiming the off-work time will be too costly. It won't be; it will be less costly and more effective.

6. We are not management consultants. We are organization consultants and just happen to have to consult through managers. But managers cause most of the problems, so we need to attack the issues (not the managers) and that means we aren't doing management consulting.

7. Accepting the diagnosis of people in the system is a bad idea. If they knew what caused the problem or what would solve it, the problem would not exist. Typically, the people with the problem had a major hand in creating it.

So what does all this mean? To me, it means that working with whole systems is what will get the best results. To do that, I have to be very stubborn about what assignments I will accept, what information I will accept, and what constraints I will tolerate. From personal experience, I have come to believe that the results possible from whole-system consulting are better in every way than trying to work on parts of systems. There is little or no recidivism and great client enthusiasm, and results can be in hundreds of percent—results not often possible any other way. This is the most exciting technology I have seen in my thirty plus years as an OD practitioner.

Kristine Quade

As practitioners in the field of change it is exciting to experience the sharing of models, how they have been modified or combined into something more robust with use. And it seems to me that the effective use of a model relies heavily on the skill, knowledge, competency, and experience of the consultant. This comes back to Bob's comment about being the instrument of change.

Bob Tannenbaum

The self is an unbelievable laboratory for learning. This, for me, stems from the notion that systems operate at all levels. So since I can look within and try to understand better what's going on inside me, what that feels like, and what doesn't work, then I can be a laboratory for all the other systems I deal with as a consultant. So we can discuss models and methods, but I believe that progress is not through better techniques and methods—I think the answer is in making better people.

Meg Wheatley

Yes, I absolutely agree with that. I think if we are more self-aware, then we realize that what happens within us is also what happens in all the other systems. That's one of the great things about living-systems theory as it applies to a person or a nation-state—the principles are the same. If we were more self-aware, we could acknowledge that everyone else is more like us than not. Then we could really start to understand each other.

• FREEZE FRAME

Take a few minutes to capture your learnings from this chapter by answering the following questions:

1. What have I learned about the way my colleagues approach the development and use of models and tools?

2. What models, methods, and tools did I see discussed here that I would like to learn more about? (See the bibliography for additional resources.)

3. What adaptations of common methods and tools did I see here that I would like to integrate into my own work?

4. How can I guard against the over-reliance on tools that some practitioners have been accused of?

5. In what ways would I want to contribute to the overall knowledge of the field in terms of the models, methods, and tools that are used?

OUR STORIES

We've been describing the stories of some conversation participants in each section. Here, we focus on a group for whom the field, when they found it, answered questions they had been asking—perhaps about how organizations operate, perhaps about how to get better results for clients.

Nancy Polend

The reason I entered the OD field was that, as I sat doing my "real job," I found myself saying things about my organization like, "It shouldn't be this way" and, "Wouldn't it be great if. . . ." I realized my purpose was to make my organization a better place: a place where the important work it was doing (conduct science in the public interest) was done by energized, satisfied, committed workers. I loved to improve things, so when I realized there was a field of study dedicated to that, I was thrilled! I am continually energized by the reality that no two organizations or situations are the same and that I must bring all of myself to every challenge, by the potential that I know exists in every individual and organization, and by the opportunities to continuously learn. If no two situations are the same and many organizations and individuals are not reaching their potential, then the opportunity to learn as an OD practitioner never ends.

David W. Jamieson

I was drawn early to really improve organizations. I saw the purpose to improve how organizations worked, how to change them and to do so in humanistic ways, and especially to improve the quality of work life for employees. Most of that is still true, only there are more stakeholders to include and care about and more values to include in the word "improve." I was always driven by learning more about what works. Over the years it also became important to worry about what's right as well. I've also always been attracted to the eclectic, multi-disciplined nature of OD and the early practitioners I learned from. A lot of OD has become more common practice and that's good (for example, participation, employee welfare, more inclusion). But along the way some humanistic values took a back seat to commercialism, profit, and power. I think good OD will always be a blend and a balancing act of good values used with good engineering, management, psychology, and process work.

Jean Neumann

At the age of nineteen, I was both a student and an employee in an alternative organization. We ran ourselves "collectively," making many important decisions together. We shared many of the same values, but fought terribly during our meetings. As we grew and became more established, our nastiness grew and become more established. I didn't understand this mess and wanted to understand. About this time, I "discovered" applied behavioral/social science in the form of week-long training workshops in group process, educational design, personal development, and organization development. I felt such relief and excitement to find a place where people could see the dynamics that I could see and had language to talk together about them.

Ann Bares

I gradually drifted into OD work from employee compensation. What propelled me into the OD arena was the realization that changing an organization's reward system has very little impact unless broader organizational issues are assessed and addressed. As I mature in my field of work—which now focuses on measuring, managing, and rewarding employee performance—I realize with increasing clarity that it is the "intangibles" (distinct sense of purpose, level of trust, communication style, and so on) that really make an organization successful. These things are more difficult to impact, particularly in today's world where speed and this quarter's bottom line are the driving principles. People have enormous amounts of passion and energy that their organizations are failing to capture. The emerging purpose of my work now is to help organizations create work that has purpose and meaning—and to match that work to the passions and values of their employees.

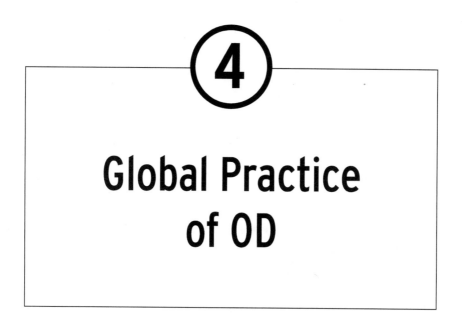

Global Practice
of OD

• FREEZE FRAME

Take a few moments to answer the following questions about working internationally before you begin this chapter:

1. What have been your observations about the practice of OD in different cultures and in different countries?

2. How does practicing OD within a global organization differ from practicing in one that is not?

3. What have you learned about what works and what does not in international engagements?

4. What are the suggestions that you have for others seeking to work on a global front? What should be paid attention to?

5. In terms of international OD, what do you wish we as a field were doing more of? Less of?

6. What advice would you give to a practitioner starting to work in your culture or country?

●　　●　　●

Global OD

Bob Tannenbaum

I would hope that, at a global level, we are paying attention to culture differences because it is so important to make sure that during the early stages there is not a violation of cultural norms. I know of many practitioners in the past who have done OD work internationally and have fallen down.

I remember teaching in Italy. My first class meeting with the students, they stood up when I came in the room. I suggested that we be more informal and that they call me "Bob." That was difficult for them; they called me "Professor Bob" instead.

Partway through the program, I offered a non-required experiment to the students. I described a sensitivity training group experience. A number really did not want to participate, and I discovered they had talked to the local priest, who thought sensitivity training was too close to going to the confessional. He would not approve the training for the students.

But it was not my job to sell them on participating. That relates to the point I have made elsewhere, and may make again, that we are facilitators, not activists. It was not my place to push those students into an American-style situation that might make them uncomfortable or at odds with their own spiritual practice.

What I also learned is that each person is, in a certain sense, like a magnet and therefore a change agent just by showing up. We have to be careful about how our intervention has impact because it is not our job to overlay our values or our beliefs on the individual or organization.

Meg Wheatley

Bob, I hear what you are saying about maintaining our neutrality with our clients, but I feel a sense of urgency. History has caught up with us. This is the first time that we know of that human beings have been capable of actually destroying the earth. I am encouraging people to start to take action on what matters to them and not sit passively by. Each individual has to notice what issues really speak to them and then put attention there. We can then rest in the knowledge that all other issues are being taken care of by others. So perhaps you might be dealing with slave labor in India. Then I can be thankful that you are working on it and I don't personally have to step forward on that issue. We do have to think about the whole, and then we need to do our own part locally.

I heard this story that relates to taking the kind of action I advocate. The story comes from Joanna Macy and her work around the world. She went to a city that lay between Chernobyl and Moscow. After the explosion, there was a cloud headed for Moscow, and the government came in and seeded the cloud. The people in that town were the sacrifice so that millions in Moscow would not be killed. She visited this city and talked with them. They said, "We just want the world to know that we did this." They didn't agree to it, but felt it could be a very meaningful act if others knew about it. What was troubling them was that the rest of the world didn't know of their action. Joanna asked, "What would you like me to tell others?" They said, "We'd like you to teach them a dance." She now has a commitment wherever she goes to tell the story and teach a dance.

To tell the story is an absolute commitment from any of us who are traveling the world. This story as it is told is more powerful than saying there is a 30 percent increase in cancer in that town.

Paula Griffin

Thanks for that story, Meg. For my part I pledge to share it with others so they can feel connected to the sacrifice those people made. Bob's story reminds me that there are probably ways in which a lot of models accepted in the United States don't translate very well when they get outside North America, or maybe they don't even make it that far.

Paul Wayne

I work in a cultural environment (Russia and Central Europe) frequently considered "unethical" in the West, and I wrestle daily—professionally, personally, and spiritually—with the content and application of differing value systems. In much of the world (outside of the United States), people live much closer to the level of survival. The higher personal principles of which we speak are sacrificed wholesale across great portions of the planet where, in practical terms, the price of a human life is much less than we would consider it to be. On the other, more positive side of the coin, the quality of some portion of human relationships against this background acquires a level of soul and intensity to which many are not accustomed.

As an example, in this paradigm, when dealing with motivation, the significance of the higher levels of Maslow's pyramid decrease in relation to the importance of a solid paycheck. The individuals who do manage to maintain their human dignity and respect for others in these barbaric conditions that exist in most places on our planet are sacred lights for the rest who would, who must (and I cannot condemn them for it) trade their principles for a piece of bread.

Like it or not, we are all lights, shining, reflecting whatever it is we are. This dialogue helps me to remember that I must not forget my role as an example before others in any instant, corner, or turn of circumstances. The eyes of truly hungry people are upon me always.

Ken Murrell

After many years doing what I felt was OD on every major continent, I have concluded that there are several points that define the field as I have experienced it practiced around the world.

First, OD is about treating people as ends and not means. This is to make the claim that we honor in our work people before all else. Counter to what others may have experienced, I do not find that we have, in this Western culture, any particular moral high ground to stand on in terms of the value of human life. I have experienced since the days I was serving in Vietnam a willingness for many to question the value of human life in another society. We can't know nor even begin to understand how life in another society is valued unless we have a very deep and real experience in that culture and many years of study. We also must be aware that valuing life is not a universal truth and, as in our own culture, there are extreme differences among many groups as to what valuing life means.

Second, to define OD as valuing people as ends can be more clearly seen in an organizational setting. Organizations serve a crucial social purpose and their production of goods and services is vitally important. Organizations serve society, and this is important to do in terms of both efficiency and effectiveness. The effort to continually develop these organizations and to treat people as ends then raises the OD challenge of how to do both when so often they appear to be in conflict.

Third, organizations and other social systems we work with as our clients are to be viewed as sustainable systems, and only if the above two values are honored is that possible over time.

Fourth, the most recent value base I believe we have come to honor is that we are truly a part of a global process and the boundaries between us and other cultures are limited and also limiting. We are in this new century global by definition. And like the proverbial fish in its water, we can't always know what our surrounding reality is unless we deeply reflect on the nature of the world that we are a part of. These are exciting times for our field. We have an opportunity to build what we call global OD, but this will be done worldwide. Our role in this is *equal* to the others in the world that feel this field should be developed.

Allon Shevat

OD, as presently practiced, is deeply rooted in Western Anglo tradition and thus basically inapplicable east of New York City or London. My attention is called to the fact that the following items, the basic fundamentals to a Western-educated OD practitioner, are certainly *not* axiomatic in places where I practice OD, that is, China, Asia South Pacific, Japan, and the Middle East:

- Teamwork and participatory management are to be valued;
- Emotions should be expressed openly, albeit "expediently";
- Managers should manage, remove obstacles, delegate;
- The consultant facilitates;
- Communication and truthful dialogue are to be encouraged; and
- Concepts like win-win should predominate.

While Western OD principles can be taught in universities and in courses, these principles cannot be promulgated in many global organizations in practice. Outside the United States and Europe, managers who rule and dictate with compassion, truthfulness, and openness are vile, rude, and upsetting of social order. "Face" needs to be maintained. Communication is opaque by design, and sharing information is foolish or treason because it negates the overriding need for total loyalty to one's boss. The boss is compassionate and the subordinate reciprocates via loyalty, shown by not sharing information with peers.

Not only are the attitudes, beliefs, and axioms different in the non-vanilla environment in which the global OD consultant works, but so is the skill set of the OD practitioner different. The global consultant needs to be able to both mediate and bear bad messages, as well as do traditional facilitating and bridge-building over cultural differences, vacillating between an expert and the OD classical facilitation role. An OD consultant may need to build relationships for months before any information of any value is gained. There will be a need to appreciate and thrive in a vague and opaque communication mode, understanding the need to drive change while saving face for the client.

Robert I. Tobin

I have learned a lot from a university colleague in Bangkok, Thailand, who is particularly effective in working with groups throughout Asia because she spends time understanding the process of change in countries where she works. She studies the culture, learns at least a few words in the language used, learns about her client's business, and understands the competitive environment for her client. When she partners with local consultants, the partnership is based on three platforms:

- Understanding of how her process skills will have to be modified in another culture;

- Knowledge of the culture and elementary language knowledge; and

- Understanding of her client's business.

Clients and consultants need a common language. When the consultant brings process skills that the client cannot understand, and the client has cultural and business knowledge that the consultant does not have, the chance for connections is not likely to be deep.

The best preparation for global work should include learning about a foreign culture and the client's business. The clients will recognize that you are someone who has made an investment in working with them.

Phil Mix

I work out of London, and my client organizations are nearly always owned (or at least controlled) by Western investors. Their leaders and OD practitioners, including nationals and expatriates, usually want me to apply what they consider to be leading Western methods to help them improve their effectiveness and performance. Often, in discussions about the consulting process to be used, they're prepared to devalue or disregard the experiences and traditions of the national culture.

During the past year, I've had a very different and challenging experience working with a large, government-owned company in the Middle East. My beliefs and assumptions about the purpose and value of organization development are being tested in unfamiliar ways as I wrestle with new dilemmas about what I stand for as a practitioner and a person. For example, what do I do with my belief in the virtues of participative democracy as I work with people who feel deep respect and near-reverence for unelected rulers who've led a country of traditional Bedouin and fishing village subcultures through a period of rapid economic and social development, opportunities, and prosperity? I have come to understand comments about the privileged places from which we Westerners often speak.

I find myself constantly revisiting, then finding ways of communicating (through actions more than words), what I believe and assume. Like Ken, I find that *treating people as ends and not means* is my most important belief or value and, ultimately, the most emotionally satisfying because of the trust of others that it appears to bring me. With a belief in respectful treatment of people as common ground, I find myself being more and more open to listening to whatever my clients have to say.

Barbara Bunker

When entering a new culture, I believe it is important to proceed with a high awareness of self. In addition, I have found that being open, warm, engaging, and excited about moving forward starts the relationship, which is the required step in cultures that develop the relationship first. From there I need to think like an anthropologist. I have to be very aware about what I don't understand about what is going on. Then I can lend myself to finding something out without forcing or affecting the situation while I figure out where they are.

I also must have a certain knowledge base about other cultures. I learned a lot from Ed Schein, who talked about the deep versus superficial culture. What shows on the surface are habits and behaviors that will immediately become apparent. The underlying deep culture is the one that shapes and forms the values. At best, when entering a system, it is important to know what social distance is expected, how business relationships are developed, when and how business can be conducted, as well as how to conduct oneself in informal situations.

I find it necessary to continually update my knowledge. It used to be we would go to Mexico to consult and just concentrate on connecting with the Mexican culture. Now there are Canadians, other Spanish cultures, and many Europeans working and living in Mexico. The different cultures are rubbing off on each other, which is both fascinating and challenging. So I read, go to school, read, study, watch videos, and ask questions. I become more knowledgeable before entering a system so as to not be insulting.

There are many OD methods that we are familiar with because they were developed in the West and may or may not transfer to other groups or organizations in other parts of the world. One of our Western OD values is participation. Some cultures don't value participation, and by presenting participation as a process or intervention, we are acting as aggressors and acting like our values are correct and theirs are not.

Most importantly, when I practice globally, I cannot have a provisional awareness. I need to check in regularly about what I think is important and draw out what is important for them. I also must take very seriously what they say and ask questions to further understand.

Bob Tannenbaum

I like the points that people are making about our international work. We also must be careful about our assumptions. We need to look at what will be helpful versus what will muddy the waters. Too often we believe that we don't have to learn the other's language; we expect them to communicate in English. We also need to be cautious of our assumption about the level of knowledge or intelligence of our clients. It may be that their training or experiences are not the kinds that make a particular intervention meaningful. For example, using clichés such as "We are on the ten-yard line and going for the touchdown" may have no meaning to someone who has never seen American football.

Sandra Janoff

Bob, I have a good story that matches what you are saying. An early experience working with native Hawaiians taught me that in Future Search we are finding our way back to ancient cultural practice. The community of Ko'olau Loa on the north shore of Oahu was seeking to reorient its approach to health care and revalidate its traditional Hawaiian values of mind, body, spirit, family, and community connection.

I was brought there to talk to a community group about Future Search. In the meeting, after hearing their stories, I began talking about the principles and methodology of Future Search. I was prepared to show a videotape, give lots of examples, and answer questions. I had barely begun when one of the planners, Auntie Malie Craver, a community elder, stopped me and said, "Sandra, we have a word in our language that describes what you are talking about." "What is that word?" I asked. "*Laulima*" she said, "which means 'it takes many hands to do a task.'" She smiled and added, "We understand what you are bringing."

In that moment I had a blinding flash. This wasn't a "new paradigm." These concepts of wholeness and inclusion weren't the discovery of 21st Century Western culture. These notions are part of a thousand-plus-year-old Hawaiian culture and, indeed, many other ancient cultures, and we need now, more than ever, to reconnect to them.

In that meeting, I also learned that every principle designed into Future Search is captured as a word or concept in the Hawaiian culture. The process of *finding common ground* is a *ho'opono*, which was an ancient practice of conflict management dating to the time when villagers could not just pick up and leave if they got into a dispute. Ho'opono means "to make things right." The Future Search was called "Ho'opono Ko'olau Loa."

This experience happens whenever and wherever we are working in cultures that have a set of basic beliefs about what gives life meaning and purpose. I have been startled, humbled, and gratified to see pictures of women dressed in black chadors standing by a mind map written in Farsi language in Tehran, Iran, talking about how to deal with street children and child abuse. Or factory workers in India squatting outside in a circle near their tire factory talking about what they are proud of and sorry about. Our guide to crossing cultural barriers is to create conditions where people can acknowledge each other and the world they live in, create a clear vision, discover collaborations they didn't know they had, make wise choices about issues of importance to them, and take effective action.

Robert I. Tobin

I have noticed that we also have to be willing to acknowledge and suspend our own cultural norms, a major effort in attempting to understand the local culture, and be diligent in using culture as one of the ways of interpreting behavior. Included would be a hyper-sensitivity to others, ability to bring diverse groups of people together, courage and risk taking, negotiation and mediation skills, deep cultural knowledge, and strength in mobilizing networks of community resources. Lack of attention to cultural rituals, discomfort with discussion of topics such as religion and family, and very different notions of formality and status are other cultural aspects that will also impact our work.

The organization development consultants who succeed in working outside of North America also have many of the same skills as effective expatriate managers and executives. They are flexible, culturally sensitive, comfortable with uncertainty and ambiguity, and are aware of the impact of their work on the local country and the entire organization.

Clients may be intrigued by specific methodologies, but their number one interest is in results. There is often pressure to accomplish objectives very quickly due to the high travel and expense costs of using consultants overseas. OD consultants who see themselves primarily as facilitators may find that additional skills, such as being a catalyst, mediator, resource locator, and bridge, are most in demand.

Jane Magruder Watkins

I have had the privilege to have "practiced" OD in nearly fifty countries around the globe. I find Ed Nicol's theories about culture are the most helpful framework. He differentiates cultures by those that are "task" or "object" focused (mostly the European male model); those that are relationship focused (African and Latin cultures); and those that are group focused (Asian cultures). While Ed acknowledges that this is gross generalization, it has been unbelievably helpful to keep in mind.

For example, in relational cultures, people are more important than task deadlines, than objects such as money and things and status. This means that those of us who live in task cultures are quick to judge relational people as not serious about work, often casual about time, and lacking ambition. Relational people see task folks as competitive, uncaring and greedy—focused on things, judging people by promptness, and meeting deadlines at the expense of their relationships.

And group-focused cultures seem to understand "wholes" and the importance of valuing the group and its wisdom. Drawing the parts into a whole through relationships precedes focus on the task. The example is the apocryphal dialogue between American and Japanese managers. Japanese: "Let's have tea and get to know each other." American: "Let's begin and we can have tea while we are working." Japanese: "Why would you want to work with someone you don't know?"

Even languages show the distinctions. For example, in English we say, "I missed the bus." In Spanish and Zulu it is, "The bus left me." Locus of control, importance of individuals as compared to groups, and the meaning of shared experience are basic elements of culture. Manifestations are seen in the food we eat, the clothes we wear, the books we read, and the way we raise our children. But no matter how much we know about each other's norms and practices, culture is about the heart—about meaning making, what matters, what is "true" for the people in that culture.

So I reached the great understanding that I could never hope to understand the gazillions of cultural norms and subcultural practices that exist on this rich globe of ours. I count it a blessing that so much of my work went all the way to the village so that the lessons got continuously reinforced. It didn't matter how much I read and questioned Americans who lived abroad about the norms of other cultures. In fact, culture is in continuous and rapid change as much as any other part of our world.

Learning about the "others" wasn't going to do it. It was myself that I needed to understand—my own culture, values, norms, and beliefs. It was about understanding that my world was only mine—not to be imposed on others but not to be denied or hidden. The more I was myself, the more others seemed to accept me. The fewer answers I had, the more I learned. And what I got was the idea that as groups form, common cultures can be created that honor differences, respect the norms of the other, and generate innovation and creativity beyond what any single culture might produce. It is our differences that are our greatest resource, our gift to each other.

Billie T. Alban

Every culture has its strengths, insights, and values. When we enter another culture, we have to recognize and honor that. When I started doing a lot of work in Latin America, I saw the strength of a "relationship" culture. I also saw that when carried to an extreme it could be smothering. However, I think the strengths outweigh the risks. When I would go to the bank in Ecuador to get a loan for our business, the bank manager would always start our conversation inquiring about my family, as I would about his. We would have a personal conversation before we switched to business. Then, he would say yes, or no, to my request. We would then move back to the relationship, at the personal level. This takes time, but in my experience it helps things along.

We have lost this in our own culture, if we ever had it. Some areas of the country may be a little better at this than others. It is important to remember that over 85 percent of the cultures in the world are relationship cultures. When we walk in, impatient to get to the point and close the deal, we are seen as pushy and crass and as not really caring about human beings, only about the task.

I loved the scene from the movie *My Big Fat Greek Wedding*. The speech the Greek father gives at the wedding sums up my own philosophy about cultural differences. He equates the origins of their family name with the word "orange" and the WASPy family name with "apple." "Hey," says the father, "here you have the apple and the orange getting married; they are different, the apples and the oranges, but in the end we are all fruit." There are wonderful differences between cultures, and, hey, we are all humans!

When I enter another culture I try to honor who and what they are, see the strengths, while recognizing who I am and what I bring. I believe it is a disservice to do as some members of the Peace Corps did, to overly identify with the new culture. They wanted to speak the language perfectly; they wanted to be accepted as a member of that culture—"go native," as the English would say. But it doesn't work. I think the host culture knows that if you can't honor the strengths in your own culture, you can't honestly value theirs.

When I first went to live in Ecuador, I would dream I was drowning. Slowly I began to recognize not only the strengths in the new culture but what I brought, an ability to make things happen, to problem solve, and to find unique solutions. We have to remember that we can honor and recognize the strengths in another culture without letting go of who we are and the uniqueness we bring. Together, the apples and the oranges can make a good team.

When I worked in Puerto Rico with a manufacturing plant, we had a goal to create a third culture (not Gringo and not Puerto Rican). We wanted to combine the best of both cultures. So we involved the whole plant. We brainstormed the strengths of the "other" culture, then talked about how to bring the strengths together to develop policies and procedures that would reflect the strengths of each culture.

One of the workers challenged the plant manager by saying, "You don't care about your family." When the plant manager asked what that meant, the response was, "Well, look at the number of hours you work. You are here on weekends and long after we have left." The plant managers laughing response was, "You sound just like my wife!" The recognition brought about some family-oriented policies in the plant.

I have a bias in my work: History is important and diagnostic. It is important to know not only the long-term history, but also what has happened recently that is part of the context for this organization. A number of years ago, when I was consulting with one of the oil companies in Argentina, the head of marketing told me he could not tell me the history of his company without telling me the history of his country and the tough times they had just been through; that's how interwoven the company issues were with the history of the country. This understanding of history and context has always been important to me, but in working in this company it was a critical success factor.

I try to keep myself informed about what is happening in the world. I read things like *The Economist* (go to Economist.com), which has the best global perspective I have found. There are excellent articles that challenge my understanding of globalization and capitalism and what is happening in different parts of the world. I always watch the BBC news because it is a different perspective than CNN. I read different kinds of books, such as *The Clash of Civilization* by Samuel Huntington from Harvard. This book was written pre-9/11 and predicted 9/11. I read about China and its approaches to economic markets. Recently I attended a conference on China. They can manufacture cheaper than we can and they have already learned all they can from us and are looking for ways to improve what they know. They may be a big market for us, but they are also, and will be in the future, a big competitor.

As a field, we are not well-read. We talk about managing differences and yet don't know about other religions, other regions of the world, other perspectives on issues. We have our own assumptions, but we are not thirsty to learn about others.

Jo Sanzgiri

I find that my practice of OD work in a global context affects me deeply, and my international work transforms me as well as the clients I am working with. I have learned that I must prepare carefully for the practice of OD in an international context. This holds true whether I work in the United States as a person whose country of origin is India, or whether I work in Southeast Asia or Latin America as a person who has chosen the United States as her country of citizenship. Specifically, I need to:

Engage in a self-reflective process. Each consultation begins with me examining my own cultural assumptions about the culture I seek to help and being aware of and accepting my biases. I need to understand the philosophy and culture of the country I am about to work in. It seems very important to realize that I live and work in the United States, and that our standard of living here is higher, different from Southeast Asia or Latin America, and that I will have to examine what it is to be an affluent American.

Focus on the context and culture of the particular area I will practice in. If, for example, I have accepted a consulting engagement in Bombay, India, I will make sure that I will have studied the latest interpretations of the *Gita* or the *Upanishads* (spiritual teachings) before I study the specific information related to the organization. Much of this information is available on websites and is easily accessible. Since India is a high-context culture, I know I will have to engage in deeply philosophical discussions during the practice of my work with senior leaders and that many interventions will have to be explained in a socio-cultural context.

Co-create the intervention strategy with the client. To do this, it seems vital that we learn the language of the culture and try to speak, even if in a nonsophisticated fashion, the few words and phrases we have learned.

Reinterpret OD models in the context of the host culture and values. While we understand the ethical norms we all practice by, these principles of practice need to be reinterpreted once we understand the complexity of the culture we practice in. Citibank in New York City will have norms and values that reflect both the culture of New York City as well as the larger American culture, but Citibank in Bombay manages change processes that are reflective of the norms of Bombay city and of India.

Integrate values of sustainability at the individual, organizational, and global levels. As we move forward after September 11, 2001, we see that cultures all around the world, especially Southeast Asian and Latin cultures, are learning to define themselves, not in relation to the United States as they once did, but looking at their own cultures, their own practices for long-term sustainability. For cultures outside the United States, my observation is that there is no going back to the idea of U.S. dominance, but learning to move forward, respecting all cultures of the world.

It seems to be a particularly challenging time to practice global OD, as if our values are being put to the test, as if we must learn to transform ourselves first, as if we must practice what *we* preach.

Kristine Quade

I am noticing a lot of comments about being prepared for global work by learning. As I have traveled and worked in other countries, I have found I learn more when I am *tolerant* enough to immerse myself within the conditions of the culture I am serving. I am humbled as I learn the importance of watering the camels and sheep before pulling up my own water from the underground well in the desert. I pay attention to how I feel without a shower for days, knowing that the Mongolians living in their Ger know this feeling is part of existence rather than comfort. I learn to not judge the Russian who goes to sleep with a bottle of Vodka next to him because the hope for a bright future is too far beyond his comprehension. It is from the "deprived" that I learn the most, as I am the recipient of their unconditional giving, kindness, connection, and life in a far more expansive way than I experience as I have been tainted by my distracters: cell phone, computer, and Palm Pilot™. I feel so wealthy when I get beyond my expectations and learn by living as others do.

Jean Neumann

What tied me up early in my career was how I agreed with and tried to follow all sorts of prescriptions about how I as a consultant and how managers should behave interpersonally. These prescriptions now make me uncomfortable, primarily because I work in Europe, where the cultural differences indicate the suitability of a variety of styles.

One principle I hold is that *I strive to leave a social system better off than when I entered.* For example, I have walked away from client systems in which it is not possible to respect basic principles of confidentiality, where I have been expected to advise executives in ways that I think result in employee exploitation, or where an approach to project management is without concern for processes of development. Even short-term interventions have to incorporate aspects of development, even if it is simply some preparation for the intervention.

I have found it painful and confusing to let go of some of the human relations norms that I had taken on through my own personal development. I am struggling afresh with what authenticity means in the absence of such norms and in a European context. I also have become increasingly convinced that OD must work in collaboration with other simultaneous change initiatives in an organization for it to be effective.

Kathie Dannemiller

I believe global work is just using common sense and primarily about getting all the voices heard in the room. This is very much a part of the culture in areas such as Thailand, India, and Africa. People there see the world as a whole system, not a bureaucratic system. So the problem may be with a linear worldview (cause and effect and old ways people were taught) and with consultants who believe they have something to tell rather than a responsibility to listen.

I go to other parts of the world with a picture of whole system work. And I have a commitment to listen to that system so that I can relate what I hear to my own understandings. I begin my work with an event planning or design team. And then begin by emptying myself out and allowing the other people in.

It does not matter where I am or who I am with. I can be in East Cupcake or in West Algeria. It is a matter of listening, moving myself out of the way, being in a place without judgment, or formulating conclusions. I look at them, eye to eye and heart to heart. I allow the essence of who each person is to come forward. I ask them to tell me about themselves, and they do! I allow everything I am hearing to permeate me. As they come into my awareness, I am literally changing. I become different because I have listened to them and they are becoming a part of my cell structure.

When done listening, I then add what I know from my own experiences and who I am into the perspective. And I know I can argue for something with great certainty because I am *them,* not *me.* This is the only way to be in order to be global. It is not about learning a new language or about their culture. It is about listening until every voice has been heard!

Lupita Martinez

I live in Mexico. I have taught OD in Mexico as well as consulted here and in other countries. There are four awarenesses that must be present for an effective connection within another culture, in no priority order:

- A deep understanding of the culture;
- Familiarity with the language;
- Being respectful; and
- Understanding the different approach to business.

When entering another culture, I have found it important to travel within the country, not just as a tourist, but living with a family, in order to know their traditions, way of life, values they respect, and the most important things to them. Develop friendships, ask questions, and be deeply exposed to the other culture.

In Mexico, what we long to have others understand is that we want to be treated as if we were important and equal to you. As a country, Mexico was conquered by the Spanish, the French, and, to some degree, the Americans. We are a country that was conquered many times. We don't want to be conquered any more. We want to be respected as peers for our special culture, ideological values, and language. It is okay for us to ask for help, but don't treat us like we are unimportant.

It is important to show respect for our traditions, religious beliefs, and ways of thinking. There are many people from Spain who live in Mexico. They have been here for many years and have become rich from their relationship with Mexico. I am very hurt when I hear them say bad things about Mexicans, such as that we are lazy or that we don't have intelligence. We are not either. We see the world through our own cultural lens, and it is important to show respect for how we view the world.

Language is only *one* barrier to understanding our culture. Words take on different meaning based on the history, context of the setting, and the relationship between the parties. For example, feedback for us is a very hard issue. Since we are a high-relationship culture, we tend to take feedback personally. Feedback about a quality or a delivery issue is often taken personally rather than as a signal to look at how to correct the fact that something is not up to expectation. Feedback needs to be given to us in a language that respects our individual talents and gifts and in a way that we can learn as peers.

Another aspect of our culture is manifested through formality, which is very complicated in Mexico. We use dress to convey the importance of propriety and respect. It is hard for us when others don't respect how important that is to us by showing up in attire that is not consistent with the situation.

I have had the opportunity to work with Spaniards, Italians, Germans, Japanese, and, of course, Americans in both the United States and Mexico. I have had to learn how to work with each of these different cultures. And I have learned that they have all expected the Mexicans to learn their ways of doing business with very little attempt at learning the Mexican way of doing business.

If the foreign business is one that follows through with their commitments, it may be difficult for them to understand the Mexican perception of time. I coach others to be clear about what they expect and follow through along the process to see how we are doing until the trust is built that both parties have a common understanding of what is expected. This needs to be done in a respectful way; be precise about expectations and provide a lot of opportunities for us to ask questions. Don't put us in the position of thinking that we are failing. That is not as respectful as helping us to understand the importance of the issue. Giving us dates for follow-up until the relationship has been cemented shows us that we are partners along the way.

We are a culture that is having to change rapidly, to move some of our culture aside in order to survive in a global economy. Some of that is good. But we still hold strongly to our relationship culture and long to have others meet us as peers as we develop business relationships.

Karen J. Davis

My recent explorations and thinking are about "global wisdom organizations," based on some of the work of the Institute of Noetic Sciences on "global wisdom society"—"a society that values all cultures and traditions and skillfully utilizes multiple ways of knowing for the greater benefit of all life."

I am still not sure what a global wisdom organization might look like. However, I believe that our major challenge is to always be looking at the wholeness, the interrelatedness, and the systemic aspects of the system. Organizations need to operate out of a deep understanding of and respect for natural systems, ancient wisdom traditions, human needs, and future generations. This includes learning from the new sciences. A global wisdom organization also trusts the dynamics of self-organizing and collective consciousness. And it is in the business of serving society and earth in life-affirming and sustainable ways.

My challenge is to help the client, whether individual or organization, to recognize their own internal wisdom, knowledge, and experiences as already providing many of their own answers. They are also the experts. My primary role is to be in service to helping them discover that expertise and wisdom in themselves and in others. I do that by creating or holding the space where people can talk/act with each other about what is important to them, to their organization, and to our world.

In many cultural contexts, ambiguity and uncertainty are a way of life. For people in other cultures, there is often a different way of thinking about and experiencing time and work. In some countries, building the relationship comes first and then the work. Time being used this way can cause us feelings of uncertainty and discomfort about not knowing and not getting to the task. We need to learn to shift to a different way of experiencing time and/or to understanding the way other people think about time.

How do we get there? One of the distinctive characteristics of our field is the art of asking questions—knowing the right question and when to ask the question. That is what differentiates us from management consultants and other change managers who may purport to know the answers. If I am truly listening, open, caring, and available to others, it is probably the "right" one—a useful question.

There is often a big difference in the focus of the practice of OD in the United States and in other parts of the world. They use OD to see the societal picture, not just the business picture. There is an eclectic consciousness or purpose. In other countries, often the primary purpose of organizations is to be "in service to others and society." In some ways competition and capitalism are not as much a reality as the human relationships, which are more important to them than money and material things. This may be more aligned with the way OD started in the United States, with people expressing more social justice values and feelings about society.

Everything I've said about working in other countries also applies to working within the multi-cultures of the United States. By my being in other countries/

cultures, I've come to know myself and my country better, and thus have become more effective in my own country of origin. I must serve by being authentic and by being aware of who I am and where I am—all within the context of being in that moment of time and space. When I deeply listen to others and myself, when I trust my intuition, and when I trust myself, my "work" goes well.

Peter Sorensen and Therese Yaeger

We believe it is important to have a framework, a conceptual framework or cognitive map, for understanding cross-cultural work. It is critical to have a cognitive map that provides a way for helping to interpret the host environment and being sensitive to our own cultural values and norms. Our experience has been that, for the global and international OD consultant to be effective, at least three factors are important.

The first factor is to have a bridge or a partner, a person who is part of the host culture and who is familiar with OD. This person helps bridge between us and the host culture, can interpret, refine, and translate what we are trying to do in a way that is acceptable to the culture in which we are working.

Second is to have what we refer to above as a cognitive map. We have found that Hofstede's dimensions of power, uncertainty, individualism, and masculine versus feminine values are central concepts in the practice of global OD.

Third is the identification and selection of OD interventions that are most compatible and most acceptable to the host culture. In our experiences, we continue to be struck by the degree of similarity of responses and stories across highly diverse cultures when describing peak organizational experiences using an Appreciative Inquiry (AI) format.

The characteristics of peak experiences appear to be common to all cultures in a way that transcends national cultural values. These characteristics include accomplishment of task under difficult conditions, which forces a strong sense of collaboration and shared efforts.

Glenn Ayres

I am aware of my work with family-owned businesses and how they function in different cultures. For two thousand odd years, progenitor governed the passage of the family estate, vineyard, or enterprise. Now, in less than half a century, everything seems to have been turned upside down. At least that's how it feels for many family businesses looking to retain their identity as private, family-owned operations.

The women had and are having their own revolution, which created massive culture change in everything from dress to inheritance laws. Now, to the chagrin of many of their fathers, these daughters want to compete with their brothers. Younger siblings no longer know their place. Give your youngest a good liberal education, an MBA from a top business school, and a stint with a major publicly held competitor, and she/he will want to compete with all your older children on the basis of "merit."

Were all that not enough, the cultural taint of globalization has impacted even some of the most traditional homegrown family enterprises. Product is now sold halfway around the world, and somehow all of us are expected to understand and make sense of the demands of not only the Americans, which is hard enough, but half a dozen other cultures who want their own variation on a product or service that has been found to be acceptable just the way it is for generations. What is a patriarch to do?

Family businesses today do have a competitive advantage over their publicly traded competitors if they can just unite the "family" around all these new mores. Their capital is patience; their planning horizons are much longer (sometimes measured in decades rather than months); and their measures of success are much more diversified. Certainly, longer-term sustainable profits are important, always have been, but so is the underlying value of their family enterprise.

So the challenge for the advisors to these businesses becomes one of helping the families to educate themselves on how to maintain and enhance their competitive position while at the same time preserving the best of their heritage. They have a head start, for there is still a strong pull in many non-U.S. business-owning families to have their children return to the family enterprise and carry on the tradition. So our job in many cases becomes one of helping the successor generation reinvent the dream of that heritage for themselves and to help them shift their own family and business cultures in a way that retains the best of the past, while making room for new demands on the business from both the competition and the highly individualistic goals of their own generation.

Cathy Royal

My work is in developing countries at the community level, most frequently in Africa. I work with small businesses that are often owned by women and with communities and NGOs focusing on sustainable development, gender equity and diversity, health care, and infant and child development. My memories and experiences reveal a renewed commitment to global organization development and change that "enhances both the consultant and the community." My commitment is to work in the world in a manner that shares knowledge in an integrated fashion. I commit to a process of social change that honors and incorporates what is good in the culture and how that can be enhanced by this organization development contact. In order to follow my commitments, I have four pillars that guide my work in this area of OD:

- Personal Balance
- Organization Development Competencies
- Cultural Sensitivity and Focus
- Social Justice Awareness

The presence of *personal balance* is most vital to my ability to sustain myself when I am working in communities and cultures that are different from mine. When I am clear about who I am in the world and what I want to contribute as the consultant and the change agent, it is easier for me to stay focused when cultural challenges arise. When I balance myself and I remain clear about what my culture has imprinted on me, I am able to see beyond or through these imprints. This balance gives me the space and flexibility to receive information and actions that can be integrated into my work and my interactions with members of this culture.

It is vital that our *OD competencies* have transitional qualities. We must be able to adapt our styles and curriculum content to shifting circumstances. If we are attached to a design or theory, we are at risk of being inflexible and operating out of our own cultural perspective, which leads quickly to inflexibility and dogma. I must know my stuff and be able to integrate it into another culture quickly and often with "low tech" tools (don't depend too heavily on the tech toys of the West). My learning over the years is that it is wise to have several theoretical frameworks from which I can pull designs and change processes.

Cultural awareness is the sensitivity that the consultant has to gender issues, hierarchy, and elder status, as well as the role of each member of a society. It is critical to providing a diagnostic that is both helpful and accurate. If I have my cultural sensitivity antennae finely tuned, my language, my intervention strategy, and my every action is threaded through this part of the practice and consultancy. I am at my best when I work with the cultural strengths of the culture and, when possible, voice theories of change and social justice that will serve the client and our desired outcomes.

Social justice is at the core of my OD practice. I work with the belief that all people have a right to access to work and systems that provide every member with opportunities for growth and success. Whether I am working with the CEO of a Fortune 500 company, the tribal chief in a small rural village, or with women in developing countries around micro business enterprise, I am clear that each system can develop opportunities for access to goods and services that increase human potential. This is for me the basis for organization and systems change. It is at the global community level that we must ask questions of social justice. This is where peace can grow; this is where understanding of culture and cooperation create the organizations and communities we deserve.

Daphne DePorres

Given the mystery factor and the accompanying reverence for those who practice abroad, I never aspired to practice internationally. In fact, I never gave it much thought until three years ago when I was offered a teaching position in an OD program at the University of Monterrey in Monterrey, Mexico. Without hesitation, I accepted the offer, sold virtually all of my possessions, packed up the kids, and headed south. I was ready for a life change much more than I craved an international experience.

From those first moments, driving into Monterrey, Mexico, in 100-degree heat with the old van full to bursting, life for me in my adopted country has been a struggle. Navigating the traffic was the first and most onerous task: cars honked nanoseconds after a light change, getting from one side of the city to another meant crossing a mountain or two, and accidentally taking those ubiquitous speed bumps at thirty-five miles an hour was no joke.

From the moment I walked into my first classroom, OD has been a joy. Students took to OD as I explained it, like ducks to water, with no indication that what we were learning was somehow culturally inappropriate. As we learned together and learned about each other, the problems, challenges, and issues seemed similar at their core. I ask my students time after time if this method or that method should be practiced differently in Mexico. I receive looks that tell me the answer is no, and why am I bothering to ask. (It bears noting here that I work in a community where OD has been practiced for over three decades and my students are often referred to the OD program by colleagues and peers who have participated in the program.)

Even though the differences did not seem apparent, after discussing this subject with another "norte-americano," we decided that the primary differences are between who we were at the beginning of our international experiences and who we are now.

Being in a culture that is foreign to us, we find that we have to work harder to be aware of the meaning people ascribe to situations and issues, to be heard, and to be sensitive to the nuances of local customs and unspoken intentions. However, the areas where we found we must pay attention actually served to help us to be more congruent with the set of OD values that we, as a group of practitioners from around the world, espouse!

I have received feedback that I am slow in learning to speak Spanish, which has created more of a struggle with my personal rather than my professional life. Language *is* a hindrance to my journey deeper into the Mexican culture, where the comforting intimacies of deep friendship and family reside.

I realize that the personal challenges are, if anything, helping me toward a greater alignment with OD values and a better use of the OD code of ethics. From the OD Credo (1996), we espouse "that human beings and human systems are interdependent: economically, politically, socially, culturally, and spiritually." As a resident and practitioner in a country that is not my own, I feel I must explore this notion or stagnate. If I adhere to the credo, I am forced to examine my values and the values of my field and to make conscious choices about standing behind these values: authenticity, openness, honesty, learning, growth, empowerment, understanding and respecting differences, synergy, harmony, peace. Back in my old home in Minnesota, I was not often pushed to examine these aspects of my adopted culture of OD.

"Is there anything different about OD in other countries?" I respectfully submit that the *essence* of the theories, methods, and approaches that each of us has learned in our home countries more than likely transcends language, local customs, laws, and norms. What might actually be different is masked. In the end, it is possible that the difference is that we, as practitioners, become different as the result of international practice and experiences, and the difference brings about a greater depth and congruence in each of us and a greater capacity to realize all that the field of OD intends.

• FREEZE FRAME

Take a few minutes to capture your learnings from this chapter by answering the following questions:

1. How has my perception of global work shifted from my answers to the questions at the beginning of this chapter?

2. What would I like to develop in order to be more effective with multinational work?

3. What principles or beliefs can I formulate that would guide my global work?

4. How would I adapt the models I use in my work and the ones discussed in Chapter 3 in order to support my principles and align with my global clients?

5. What can I contribute to global OD?

OUR STORIES

A surprisingly large group of people happened upon OD quite accidentally on their way to other careers, attracted by what the field offers. It's interesting to notice the variety of careers from which we have been diverted.

Jonathan Ross

I came to OD through working as a lawyer-manager in the public sector, faced with an underappreciated staff whom I could not reward financially due to municipal budget constraints. I wanted them to feel valued and to be given a chance to make their best contributions, so we had to work on creating a culture change in the organization, or at least in our little corner of it.

Nancy Roggen

I entered OD without knowing I was doing so—helping a steel service center move from paper-and-pencil to automating our ways of working. It was appealing to help people to do more meaningful work: working with the customer, not the paper; having a more complete sense of their work, rather than working on small, seemingly unrelated tasks; seeing how what they did connected with the customer and with others in the organization.

Patricia Firestone

I was working as a new-graduate registered nurse and was offered a position as head nurse of five very busy clinics in a large teaching hospital in Los Angeles. There was no orientation to the role, no training or development offered to me as a new manager, and no mentor. After eighteen months of frantic paddling in this "toss her in the pool and see if she swims" environment, I drowned. Now, as an individual consultant, my goal is to never forget how it felt to be that new clinic manager, so unprepared to contribute to the organization, so ready to be another casualty of a system that did not recognize individual growth and development needs and the impact of that on overall organizational effectiveness.

Jane Magruder Watkins

I began this incredible journey almost by accident. During the Carter administration I was the internal OD person on the staff of the Action Agency—at that time it was made up of the Peace Corps, VISTA, and the Older American Volunteer Programs. Some sticky issues in the Peace Corps took me to southern Africa. It was the beginning of a journey that has been a blessing in my life beyond imagining.

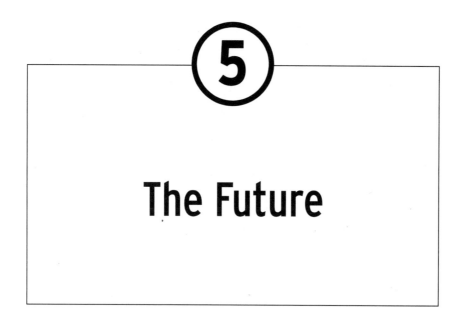

The Future

• FREEZE FRAME

Take a few moments to answer the following questions so that you have a grounding of your own thoughts about the future before you begin this chapter:

1. What are your hopes, concerns, and wishes for the future of OD?

2. What shifts are you noticing in the world where you work? Are there trends or possibilities emerging, either at macro or micro levels?

3. What do you see in the future of organizations and business?

4. What do you see as the greatest needs for the future in terms of practitioners' purposes, values, models, methods, and skills or competencies?

•   •   •

Future Focus

Bob Tannenbaum

As we begin to consider the future, I'd like to go back to the suggestion that we have some choice as individuals. We have power to change the world. In the early years, we did not lay out a grand strategy for the field, for ourselves, or for change. It was a step at a time and looking for opportunities. A lot can happen if one doesn't see the system as an enemy and fight it. If one has a good sense of the system and ways it works, a sense of readiness of different parts of the system to at least look at something differently, then change can happen. Part of the strategy as I see it for the future is looking ahead to see how we can get more and more people who can actually confront the madness that is out there, rather than accept it.

Meg Wheatley

Bob, I envy where you were in the beginning of the field. You were really creating something new. I have a need for many people now to know what it feels like—to be in a revolutionary band where you're not fighting the system; you're actually eagerly engaged in creating something. That experience is unlike any other. We need more of those people who are willing to confront the madness. And we need them to find each other. When we find each other, that's when our power emerges into something very different.

In my own work I'm no longer trying to fix the old. We may be facing a completely unpredictable catastrophe, and there is nothing that I or anyone else can do to stop the disintegration. As a conscious human I can see that it is not going to work if we continue in this path. It is very scary, and I believe that it's necessary for things to come apart. Something profound has to shift. The only thing we have to concentrate on is new ways of being, and we have to put our best energy into creating the new.

Robert (Jake) Jacobs

For me, Meg, that "act of creation" is the single most challenging work that lies ahead for us all. An easy way out is to fight against others who do not share our beliefs and values. The much harder path is to confront their (and our own) assumptions and beliefs in a way that is creative, not destructive. When we're standing around the metaphorical coffee pot talking about how "they" don't get it or writing books about a better way that we know but "they" don't, we're not just creating something. We're simultaneously working to destroy something (or someone) else, whether we are intentional or conscious about it or not. I believe our challenge for the future is to draw circles that include others—especially those whom we consider "they"—those who don't readily share our beliefs and values. When Bob talks about connectedness, this is what deep connectedness is about.

David Sibbet

I have always remembered that the field of OD found inspiration in the work of open systems theory—inspired by the work of people like Ludwig von Bertalanffy on living systems. Perhaps nature herself is a guide to our future. Nature renews itself in simple, direct ways. Things that learn how to reproduce and thrive within their niches reproduce more and evolve into the complex, beautiful systems we all admire.

Nature's mechanisms of mitosis, seeding, producing eggs, and reproducing life can be adapted by OD to provide a spectrum of tools. We spread what works when people move to new settings and share what they know. We spread hope and life when we publish and create tools that have all the ingredients people need to recreate our processes and effects in the new "soil" of another situation. Our stories are the DNA. Our process guides are the seed packs.

When we conduct our workshops and hold our seminars, in person and online, we are creating a space for the possibility of new understanding, eggshells of possibility for new chicks. When we personally take apprentices under our wings and create companies and practices that are in fact wisdom schools, we participate in direct birth. I trust these ways of nature more than the egoic plans of minds disassociated from the natural world.

Seeding our knowledge of whole systems, of living systems, of evolving, dynamic, and regenerative systems may yet leaven the hard clay of mechanistic understanding. Some of us will work inside large organizations with immense resources. Others will prefer the niches in the thin soils of less fortunate places. Some of us will spread on the winds, and others of us will burrow. I like to think that OD's genius is its resistance to definition, its blooming diversity, its spaciousness of vision, and its embrace of nature. We aspire to emulate nothing less than life itself. And life, as many of us know, is resonantly in touch with itself. In the collective impact of our small acts of sharing I find hope.

Linda Ackerman Anderson

I have two themes I am tracking: (1) leverage and (2) connection/relationship/co-creating. About leverage, I think about the level of intervention we focus on (individuals/pieces versus enterprise-wide/larger systems; immediate goal versus long-term impact), the influence level of our client (manager/worker versus executive/influence leader of whole systems and processes; behavior/skill versus mindset/consciousness), and creating a plan versus building an integrated strategy.

It is not my intention to put a value load on these either/or examples. All of this work is valuable. And for me, if I can only do so much, if I only have the time I have, I would much rather focus my practice on interventions that leverage change, the larger systems, deeper personal work (mindset), longer term impact, and continuously adaptive/improving/self-reflective processes.

About connection/relationship/co-creating: I love our community and the fact that we talk, relate, and really listen to each other about what is most important to us and our impact on the world. My truth is that I wish at this very moment that I were having this very conversation, or at least a conversation of this content magnitude, with senior leaders who are in positions to influence the mindsets, culture, work, and outcomes of the thousands of people in their organizations.

These conversations are great models of the depth of connection, the quality of the thinking/feeling/listening required of relationships that we must create with our clients . . . so that we are not just talking, but are really connecting and being moved and personally altered to be and live co-creatively. I would love us to play on organizations' goals to increase their global "connectivity" so that connectivity is not just electronic, but is human . . . is relationship—to co-create together for the good of all. I know my work for the future will have a core purpose of building and modeling the quality of relationship, connection, and co-creating that produces outcomes that are both humane and of lasting *leveraged* value for the world.

Aurelie Laurence

I agree, Linda, about leverage and leadership. I have experienced an organization that was run by a leader who had wonderful participatory values and who failed because of his introversion and the fact that the people working for him wanted, not participation, but orders. I am not suggesting we throw out participation. We need to keep everything we've done that has moved us forward. But we are entering a new time that needs new thinking and guidance from those who can see above the fray. We need to put the seers in leadership. They will use the various strategies we've already discovered and start demonstrating new ones that we can only then begin to describe.

It appears as if the people who have the kind of leadership ability we need for the future are not always, or even often, in positions to lead. They might be what we call the informal leaders. But the smaller or larger culture stops them, so they move quietly, looking for openings. What do we, as purveyors of organizational wisdom, have to offer the real leaders whom we need to emerge in the cultures in which they stand? How do we find them, anoint them, support them, and follow them? Maybe our job is to make the openings.

Nancy Polend

I believe OD is on the verge of great opportunity and impact. Because it is getting harder and harder for organizations to thrive in the rapidly changing conditions of our time using Industrial Age organizational structures, behaviors, and strategies, OD is uniquely positioned to help. Modern organizations are struggling to do new things under always-new conditions with old systems. Hierarchical structures and behaviors, which were appropriately designed in response to the stable conditions of the time (1900 to 1940) are no longer sufficient in the dynamic conditions of today.

As OD has evolved, it has been focused on incremental change: planned, discrete, and measurable changes. It used to be that we could go into an organization, do a diagnosis, propose a change, implement the change, and sit back and see whether the change "fixed" the problem. If not, then we'd try something else, mostly with the luxury of time and study, money and safety. Although OD has always advocated for changes with humanistic foundations, the demands for making such changes were ad hoc in a time where most everything organizations did resulted in prosperity, or at least effectiveness.

Today, as we know, it is another matter altogether. Organizations are starting to feel urgency about making the changes necessary to create the nimble, always-learning, innovative, and flexible organization it takes to survive and thrive in today's dynamic environment. The pull toward these characteristics has been increasing over the last twenty years and is now, I believe, at the "tipping point."

The principles that OD professionals have always used and the types of changes we have historically facilitated have finally matched the type of environment that more acutely needs them. Before, the types of changes we facilitated were "nice to have." Now, they are "must haves." It's as if the OD answer we've always had has finally found the conditions we needed to make the kind of impact we always knew we could make. I believe organizations are being naturally (and urgently) pulled to the kinds of changes OD has always supported; it is no longer avoidable. OD has always had so much to offer and now, I believe, it will finally get the chance to change the world.

Ron Carucci

Not to be a totally dissonant voice, but I want to offer a bit of a provocative perspective here. If we invited any CEO or senior executive in any of the organizations to join us in this conversation and said to him or her, "This is what I believe my field should aspire to; could you please comment?" what do we believe he or she would say, having read our collective commentary? My strong hunch is that he or she would look quite crossed-eyed at us.

While I am moved by the thoughts of a greater need for connectedness and the opportunity for greater relevance, have we truly found a way to reach those men and women who are the ones who *actually will* change the organizations in which we practice? They, *not* we, are the ones who must lead great revolutions, create greater meaning for those they lead, and, ultimately, find ways to sustainably bring about change. It is *they* we must find deeper connection with. It is *they* who must find relevance in our work, not us. Do we speak their language? Are we credible to them in the context of the complex, dynamic, challenging, broken worlds in which they lead? Do they look to us as meaningful and helpful sources of advice and support to them, or do they look at us and think we are living in our own world, far apart from theirs? (That's been the rap on the OD field, and I fear, still is).

I believe Nancy is right—now more than ever, we can have impact. My wish for our future is that we will be *credible* partners to the leaders we serve. That we will be seen as fresh thinkers with relevant advice and capabilities to help them transform the enterprises they lead into not only what is meaningful to us (spiritually balanced and healthy workplaces), but what is meaningful to them (profitable, thriving, growing, competitively superior, and high-performing enterprises). These are *not* the polarities we have long treated them as—they do go hand-in-hand, and the leaders we consult with have never believed we see that. Now is the time for us to show them we understand their worlds and that we are capable of meeting them where they are, coming alongside them in *mutual pursuit* of one another's organizational aspirations.

Edith Seashore

While I recognize that all problems are system problems, there is nothing to the work system if the human system is taken out. Maybe the root of the whole problem is that some are using human terminology and others are using systems terminology. We are not listening to each other and are working hard to make a distinction between this or that.

The early founders were curious about anything that had a relationship to what was being done. They were looking at what parts could be put together rather than for distinctions. Everything that came along was looked at, not as something to be distinguished, but to be incorporated in some way or in a different kind of order.

We have shifted from a field of conceptualizers to a field of practitioners. Because of that, there is an attempt right now to delineate rather than incorporate. Because of "ownership of the practice," we may be changing the titles of some things rather than exploring them in relationship to the whole field of OD.

I have noticed that the big consulting firms are quite successful at rearranging things but we, as OD practitioners, seem to be called in to clean up the mess after they have left. If all we have done has led us to where we are now, it is scary. Is this all the progress we have made?

Our new practitioners are not getting the basic training in psychological methods, such as working in groups or how people change. However, they may be getting training on what the new OD is! Maybe graduate programs would be a good place to focus on helping to "reboot" the field.

Diana Whitney

One of our future tasks is in co-creation. If we care about the well-being and preservation of humanity, we can challenge our beliefs about change, resistance, and the core processes that are getting in our way and begin to influence from a positive core.

First, if we challenge our beliefs by asking deficit questions (what is not working), then deficit gets the attention. If we ask questions that are choicefully affirming and life giving, we will understand what excites or enlivens creativity for people.

Second, we know that who is there in the room at that moment is creating the future. So getting all the stakeholders in the room is important, and the larger the better. As Meg says, we need to be in conversation. The impact of the conversation is what holds us together. It is humanly satisfying. When we explore with language, using the vocabulary of relationship, community, and network, we are the human system, not just "the system."

For me, the future of the field of OD is that we must grow beyond the roots of small-group methodology and expand the capacity to create large-scale change and transformation.

John Adams

It seems to me that we cannot go on much longer in a "business as usual" mode. Challenges arising from the continued rapid expansion of the global population (mostly poor), the continued accelerating disparity in wealth around the world, the continued degradation of the environment, and the continued "take-make-waste" paradigm of consumerism are creating ever fewer choices for both individuals and organizations.

I am certain that in the very near future (even today) there will be/is a huge call for conflict work, creativity, networking and alliance building, re-establishing humanistic values and preserving individual dignity, developing broader and longer term perspectives, scenario building, systems thinking and system-based diagnoses, ethics/social responsibility, and so on—all part of the core work of OD.

In sum, I do not think we can have any doubt that, to a large extent (barring cataclysmic asteroid hits and the like), the form of the "future" will be strongly influenced by organizational actions. I believe the only choice is whether or not to exert this influence consciously or to take what we get by not paying attention. If OD is to have a viable future, I believe that it must once again become interdisciplinary—understanding what economics, systems dynamics, ecology, populations studies, policy research, and so on have to say about the situations we are drawn to address.

Frederick A. Miller

I believe that OD will play a critical role in the survival of organizations. Our basic premise—that organizations should allow humans to be human—is becoming thoroughly integrated in many organizations around the world.

The future of OD is strongly connected to its past. Up to this point, the OD field has mostly been priming for the new era that is just dawning, an era in which the world has bought the basic premise that work environments must be created where humans can be human and everybody can do his or her best work. Organizations need new behaviors, new solutions, and new systems for making this new work culture a reality—work that may take the next fifty to sixty years.

This means that organizations are going to become increasingly disconnected from their pasts. The old ways—the hierarchies, the expectations, the reward systems, the management models—have become extraordinarily obsolete in just the past two decades.

Tomorrow's generation of workers will approach their organizations in a new way. They will expect organizations to accommodate their full selves; they will not sacrifice certain aspects of their identities to be accepted. They will also want to be part of organizations that are aligned with their own values, organizations that are worthy of their commitment and passion.

Even organizations that do not yet see the value of diversity and inclusion will either be forced to do so soon or risk survival. Undeniably, our country—and our world—is becoming increasingly diverse. Inclusion must follow if organizations want to leverage that diversity and create an environment that enables higher performance. This will require a huge culture change for most organizations, and OD will be the key to facilitating that change.

Jane Magruder Watkins

I agree that the work of OD is helping human systems create their own unique ways of honoring and embracing differences, learning how we can find those common dreams, those higher purposes that bind us as the human race while honoring the differences.

Because of my interest in global organizations that value the complexity of the world and embrace the chaos of creativity, I know that Appreciative Inquiry (AI) thrives in multiplicity, in radical democracy when all voices are heard, in the realization that the world we create by the conversations we have is a choiceful act. AI gives us a perspective that moves beyond a compulsion to create order that is predictable, plans that last for years, and managers who are taught to lead through mechanistic methods. I understand anew the wisdom of the founders of NTL—that the first and most continuous task of a change agent (an OD practitioner, if you will) is to commit to personal continuous learning and growth. We project onto the world around us all that exists within us. The good news is that we have choices about what is "within" us and how we understand and act on that reality.

Day Piercy

If we believe that organizations' future success requires them to become self-organizing systems, then we must stop offering the traditional consulting services that organizations know and expect from us. So I believe that the OD consulting field needs to die so that a whole new field with its center inside organizations and communities can rise. This death of our field is a logical and creative outcome of the rise of self-organizing theory and practice.

In the past, we were able to work with organizations to develop a plan they could then implement. We were careful to stay outside of the organizations' cultures in order to be the external resource they needed—to provide an external perspective and to be a facilitator for negotiation and conflict resolution. At times we also have provided research and analysis and developed specific recommendations or alternatives to solve problems and to build successful organizations.

Now, as organizations face complex challenges, information flooding, and fast-paced change, we know they need to be self-organizing systems that can weave throughout the organization, innovating and implementing, learning and creating continuously at all levels internally and externally.

By definition these services place us outside the organization's self-organizing system. If we agree to be the external consultant that organizations request, we will become the brick wall that prevents the very breakthroughs they seek. We will be the source of their failure. We cannot succeed as consultants because we will have contributed to weakening their self-organizing systems.

My solution to this conundrum is that we consultants destroy our field as quickly as possible. Stop offering the traditional consulting services. Tell organizations that the old approach will not give them the results they seek. Nature teaches us that transformation always builds on what exists already and our current strengths. We can focus on the new snake emerging or on the old skin that is being shed. We must create a new field that mirrors nature's form. We must connect consultant self-organizing systems with the self-organizing systems of the groups we serve.

Helene Uhlfelder

Day Piercy's point of view is interesting. Having left OD work for several years so that I could learn more about technology and how organizations were adapting to the Internet, I experienced clients that had thrown organization development and organization design out, along with most forms of teams, participation, and quality programs. At the same time, I saw clients who had brought the external consulting model and external consulting in-house, which was a good thing.

However, there are still organizations that need help in transforming the business or organization into something that can continue to grow and thrive. I believe many of the methods we have used over the last twenty years are still valid in some form. They may need to be modified to align to the current economic conditions and the higher skill levels of people in organizations, but we should not abandon them.

The idea of systems thinking and alignment of strategy, process, technology, people, and organization are just as important today as they were years ago. Yes, we need to modify our approaches some, but the basic tenets for how organizations function are still worthy of consideration.

I am very interested in what comes next and believe that it should be built on the best of what we know works and that we should not give up on these methods just because they may not be as popular as in the past.

Chris Worley

When I think of the death of OD, the strategist in me wants to spin out alternative scenarios based on a set of economic and market trends and value dilemmas such as:

- Globalization of commerce and work;
- Increased infiltration of technology in all aspects of life;
- More diverse, educated, and contingent workforce;
- More networked organizations;
- Increased conflicts between positivism versus social constructionism;
- Increased conflicts between values of performance versus process;
- Increased conflicts between values of egalitarianism versus concentrated wealth; and
- Increased interest in ecological sustainability.

These scenarios are not intended to be mutually exclusive or independent. On the contrary, the future of OD no doubt will be some combination of these. For me there are three scenarios; each, in its own way, is controversial. Depending on which trend becomes predominant and most influential over the field of organization development and change, it may become "OD as agent for humanism at work," "the profession of change," or "change as academic discipline."

OD As Agent for Humanism at Work. In this scenario, the field returns to it root values and they are clear, relatively few, and shared. There is a strong culture among OD practitioners about the purpose of the work. In fact, these values take on the status of objective and outcome. The purpose of the field is to bring spirit, passion, and human integrity into the workplace. The focus of the field is value promulgation, to humanize work and organizations, to bring work-life balance into the forefront of conversation, to sponsor and champion diversity and spirituality. In essence, OD "holds on" as a distinct field and crafts an identity separate from "change management." It is relatively small (compared to other applied fields of change), but vigorous.

In this scenario, practitioners are focused on process in all of its varieties (or vagaries) and eschew discussions of relevance or performance issues because they believe that attention to process is enough of a goal in itself to warrant effort and that performance, while important, is too narrow a pursuit. Such an orientation supports goals and values of egalitarianism and works to decrease the concentration of wealth in society. This perspective argues that organizations should be very concerned about doing the "right" things and being agents of social change and corporate citizenship. Therefore, conversations built on change principles of social construction and ecological sustainability are legitimate actions.

The Profession of Change. In this scenario, the focus is on practice and there is a bias toward performance over process, toward outcomes of the work. The central value is performance—the golden ring—and process is important because it represents a strategy to achieve performance. With its focus on practice, the design and implementation of interventions occupies most of the practitioner's day; how can change practice, theory, and concepts be used to help organizations adapt? Relevance is the watchword of these professional practitioners, and what works is their mantra.

In this scenario, globalization and technology trends dominate, performance values are prepotent over process values, and the concentration of wealth may be seen as an unfortunate side effect of effective organizations (although, increasingly, networked organizations may moderate that effect). These conditions suggest that the field is captured by the phrase "organization change"—that OD as we know it today is an historical footnote. The profession is characterized as relevant and balanced, but applied practice. That is, its focus is on consulting, helping managers and organizations manage change and adapt, building capacity to manage change, and other practical issues.

Compared to the previous scenario, the focus of attention shifts to issues of theory and practice, and the characteristics and value orientation of the consultant become less salient. Relevance, a small voice in the prior scenario, takes center stage in this scenario. Practitioners in the field are business savvy, view individuals (and themselves) in instrumental terms, and pursue relevant change processes and their development as ends in themselves.

Change As Academic Discipline. Here the focus is on the evaluation of change in organizations. As a result, performance and process are equally important because the focus is on the understanding, prediction, and control of the organization change process. This perspective is more distant from the subject of change. It is more concerned with generalizable conclusions about how change occurs, how it is triggered (by globalization, technological change, powerful elites, and so forth), under what conditions it works well, and so on. Under this scenario, the "OD as profession" scenario dies out because OD and change management practices are embedded in the line manager's responsibilities. The academic scenario is unconcerned with whether an OD practitioner was involved, except as an explanation of why change occurred and whether it was helpful in producing specific outcomes.

Michael Mitchell

I think our field is ready for a serious change. We have moved forward for forty plus years as an all-including and values-focused bunch. It has been a great few decades. However, we haven't competed well as a field with the big accounting firms, which have decided that they are in the change management business. Instead, many in the field have fractionated into ever more esoteric product groups, selling products instead of consulting help.

We have continued to act like behavioral scientists, rather than as organization specialists, and have largely ignored the technology side of organization life. The net is that we are stuck in the box of being a "soft" product rather than a results-oriented profession. Somehow, we have also become mixed up about what is developmental for us versus developmental for the client.

The problem and the answers are undoubtedly hitting us right smack in the face. I think we need to stop and think about our mid-life crisis and decide who we want to be if we grow up. There is a huge need for good OD consulting; we just have to learn how to deliver it, and market it, and how to deliver real value. We have the skills within the profession to do this, but it will take a bunch of us working together to pull it off.

Billie T. Alban

I want to start with the present. We are going through some difficult times right now. Many external consultants are finding it hard to get work. Internal consultants are fearful of being laid off. With business working at the survival level in terms of the Maslow hierarchy, many things that we offer are put on the back burner. We are a superfluous service to organizations unless we can help them see the value we bring.

I think we need to know what is happening with our clients and customers. We need to focus on how we can help them in this economy; we may have to put some things on hold until the economy changes. We know how to help with change and transitions. We know how to listen to issues and concerns and then work with others on creative solutions. This is the kind of help we can bring. We need to be as customer-focused as possible.

Where there is some interesting work going on is in the public sector. Many different agencies are using whole systems approaches to work with clients and customers. This may not pay as well, or at all, but it is an opportunity to work with democratic processes around citizen involvement for the common good.

Now, on to trends that I see that may influence the future. I think we need, in our society and our businesses, more stakeholder involvement in key issues. The stakeholders may be customers, suppliers, employees, clients, or citizens, but we are going to use and see developed processes for stakeholder inclusion and participation. I was struck over a year or so ago when George Schultz was being interviewed on PBS about the Arab/Israeli issue. He said, "The biggest mistake we made was at the first Camp David talks; we didn't have all the stakeholders at the table!" (I don't know if they could have gotten them all.) "The assumption that we made was that if you have the two leaders, they represent the others." They did not have the system in the room! I think, whether face-to-face or electronically, we are going to see more involvement and participation. It is going to require constructive processes and creative management. Of course, the critical issue that we are all aware of is that we desperately need better ways to deal with conflict, polarities, major differences. I hope that in the future we will find methods that help in these areas.

As Barbara Bunker and I have talked to practitioners about their work, we have found interesting and innovative approaches people are using, creative adaptations of other approaches. The problem is that there is no forum to learn about these individual creative approaches. I suppose the National OD Network Conference is a place where some of this happens, but I think a forum, less formal, where people can gather and tell stories about what is working, what they are doing, what they have invented, would help all of us. This has always been a field where we learn from each other and build off of each other's ideas.

W. Warner Burke

A current paradox that does not bode well for the future is the strong need for security—job security, organizational survival, and environmental safety (terrorism, ecological damages, and so forth)—while at the same time there is just as strong if not a greater need for risk taking, innovation, and creativity. In the face of trying to protect our organizations and ourselves, we need to be fostering experimentation, rapid change, and getting ourselves out of comfort zones. Isn't it possible for us as consultants to help people to feel safe enough to take risks?

A point about the future is our need to understand as clearly as possible that *complexity* is the new reality. Everything seems to be more complicated today. We have to deal with competing values, with organization change that requires multiple simultaneous interventions, and with people who still believe that OD is "soft stuff"—an absurd belief. So we must learn much more about and rely much more on complexity theory, nonlinear complex systems theory, and chaos theory. And we must practice what we expect of others—that the game we are in demands a value of lifelong learning.

Glenda Eoyang

My work in the complexity sciences encourages me to think of this field in terms of "dynamics" rather than "development." Human systems dynamics encompasses many of the foundations that Bob Tannenbaum considers necessary to this emerging field, and it transcends the identity crisis we are encountering as organization development professionals.

"Development" implies an end-determined state. The individual, the team, or the organization as a whole is assumed to be moving through a developmental process from the immature past to the more mature (and presumably more perfect) future. In this state, our job is to help clients determine their preferred states, design and implement interventions to move them and their organizations toward the goals, and evaluate their performance and ours against some imagined standard. When we frame our work in this way, we believe a more perfect future state can be defined; we assume that there is one "best" developmental pathway; we force ourselves to choose between the development of the individual and the development of the institution; and we find ourselves caught in the tension between elitism and democracy.

Complexity science offers a different way to think about change in highly diverse and loosely coupled systems called "dynamics." Dynamics describes change through time, but it invokes a different set of assumptions and connotations than "development" does.

Complex dynamics are not end-determined. No predetermined path shapes the emerging behavior of the individual or system. Rather, the significant differences in each moment play themselves out and evolve into something entirely new. This image of change is sometimes referred to as dialectic. Two engage as opposites, and something new comes to be. The synthesis cannot be predicted, but when it does emerge, it becomes the foundation for the next engagement and the next generation of dialectic transformation.

When we think of our work as dynamic rather than developmental, many of the challenges that confuse us today are transformed into rich opportunities for learning and growth. Differences that appear to threaten our sense of self and field become differences that feed our individual and collective growth. Many of the tensions that we describe can be seen as such fertile paradoxes, rather than as threats to the integrity of the field.

We wonder whether we should close the field to the overconfident neophyte and rely on the knowledge elite of the past to define the field. Human systems dynamics would lead us to believe that both the learner and the learned have powerful resources to contribute and that keeping them engaged with each other will lead to healthier, more resilient theory and practice.

Sandra Janoff

I am aware of the power of differences and the following contradiction: Systems develop when they can recognize and make use of differences. A system that can discover and use its resources, skills, and capabilities is a more mature working system. But *we human beings don't like differences.* We see something that is different and we immediately want no part of it. We bully, decide we are better than they are; we alienate, coerce them to change; we ignore, treat them like they have a problem; and on and on. We stereotype and scapegoat. So instead of having a society where we appreciate our functional differences, we have a society that feeds on its stereotypic differences. How's that for negative and depressed?

I see that our job as facilitators is to pay attention to the differences that surface during our work and ensure that scapegoating does not occur. When someone says or does something that stands out as different, putting him or her at risk of being out on a limb alone, we ask a question that is counterintuitive. We ask if anyone else is feeling the same way. Then the difference is joined and validated and the emotional energy becomes less charged. That is how we manage to keep systems whole.

Jacqueline Byrd

I am focusing my attention on a smaller group within organizations in order to grow and leverage their resources. They are innovative, creative, risk takers and they see the need for change. They understand how to communicate and empower themselves and others. Often, however, they're isolated in pockets within the organization. You put them together and the sparks fly, the ideas fly, and a group that wants changes to happen becomes a moving force.

Edith Seashore

Let me add three things I believe OD needs. First, we need to improve our use of technology, to learn how to incorporate technology into our approaches. Six Sigma, for example, is a technology approach, and as a process it needs to include getting people to work together more effectively—an OD approach. Those in technology need us and we need them. The two are not together right now.

Second, we might learn to be more politically savvy. We do not know how to work effectively with those individuals who make political decisions. We know how to work with the organizations after the decision has been made. However, politics operates regardless of how effective the organization is functioning. This may mean that we have to turn our attention to working at the grassroots level, rather than trying to reach the top.

Third, we need to learn what it means to be part of a global society. We have become very "Americanized" and will need to learn to understand and deal with real diversity, real conflict.

Kathie Dannemiller

I believe we are not going to be doing anything new or different in the future. I believe we will be doing what is ordinary common sense. Our roots were community work—letting each person's voice be heard. There is power in community. Community used to be defined as a geographical neighborhood. But now community could be a group, organization, listserv, virtual team, or a topical conversation group. It could be anything if we seek to define community in different ways. There is power in connecting with others whom we may never meet, but the voices get heard. Imagine the power of sending a politician a single email versus being a part of fifteen thousand other emails sent with the same focus.

People are feeling more powerless, frustrated, and isolated. I need to feel that I am connected to others who have common yearnings. If I can hear others, see them in my mind's eye, or feel that I matter, then I am powerful. Interestingly enough, this is what the founders of this nation were about—to ensure that every voice was heard! That is powerful community work and the future of OD.

The secondary piece for me is that the "old timers" are passing on and indeed should be helping the next wave of practitioners. In the early days of NTL, we would simply open our hands to each other. What comes to mind is the song: "Love is nothing until you give it away, and then you end up having more. Have a magic penny, hold it tight and then don't have any." The principle of NTL was to give it away. We did not worry about trademarks or that someone could steal our thoughts. We were about sharing, expanding, and wholeness. So my hope for the future would be to open your hands and let everyone have it; don't hold it tight.

Bob Tannenbaum

I agree with Kathie. The early practitioners were few and the academics were many. Now that has reversed. There is little research or new ideas (as against new practice methods) being developed by the academics. There were not many new ideas until New Science came along. But I believe this is just an evolutionary (rather than revolutionary) theory. OD came from the other sciences before it came into the people area. We always emphasized the existence of systems, subsystems, and supersystems and interdependence and connectedness of the parts.

Perhaps if we keep opening the door to other fields, we will realize that, given the billions of years of existence of the universe, there are still similarities that we keep encountering. Rather than thinking we are a highly complex system, we will discover that the beauty is that the processes are quite simple. The difference is not in the repeating process but in the amount of time that a process takes.

Bev Scott

We have to think of our core practice as a living system that can be adaptable to the needs of organizations, the world, and our clients. We did not have complex adaptive systems in mind in the 1960s with the emergence of T-groups. Yet, the application of our methodology is more complex. Team building and small-group work have moved to large groups and flexible and adaptive processes for the alignment of culture, strategy, and the human system.

We need to learn how to use various tools at multiple levels of the organization while paying attention to the impact, influence, and interaction our methods can have at all levels of the system. We must pay attention to the complexity of our world and be the voice of humanity and inclusion, rather than be driven by interventions that support rigid structures, command and control, alienation, and such gross inequity. There is not enough stability in today's organizations to offer certainty. We can, however, offer a systemic perspective and a view that provides a comfort zone or reassurance so that there can be movement to a new place while in the midst of chaos. Therefore, OD as a field must continue to hold the humanistic values and the foundation of participation, learning, and involvement.

Meg Wheatley

This reminds me that "self-organization" has two words in it, and both describe a process that we then trust. We can trust what the process is, and that everything that comes into form is a result of decisions or of choices Those choices are influenced dramatically by our beliefs and values. So if you want to change an organization and an individual, then you have to uncover those core beliefs and values and expose them, bring them to the light of day.

That's usually a pretty horrifying experience for people in organizations because they may have thought they were people of integrity or people with compassion and generosity. They now suddenly realize they've been acting like the most revengeful, most deceitful group together. But then you choose new values. You try to create new values, new processes, new relationships based on those values. That's why I think values (and I mean that in a broad way because I'm throwing beliefs in there also) are the fundamental place where change happens or not.

Ken Hultman

My attention right now is on what you are saying, Meg. What troubles me is the insidious growth of organizational mistrust and the implications that this holds for the future. Trust is a fundamental condition for personal, interpersonal, and organizational effectiveness. The opposite of trust is fear, which crushes the human spirit. Trust is rooted in the belief that you can really depend on other people. Organizational trust has been in a free fall during the past twenty years. The decline was ushered in by the surgical use of downsizing and restructuring to cut costs. This has been exacerbated in recent years by the seemingly neverending revelations about corporate wrongdoing and corruption. Then you can add to this the impact of technological advancement, ad hoc, and virtual teams, which have served to make interpersonal relationships increasingly impersonal, superficial, and transitory. The average worker now feels terribly alienated, wondering, "What do I have to do to survive?"

As humans we are basically social in nature, and the workplace is a primary venue for meeting our social needs. A sense of belonging enhances productivity and morale, but this has suffered greatly due to the almost obsessive emphasis on short-term profits and speed-to-action change. Healthy interpersonal relationships require face-to-face interactions over a period of time, which is how we develop rapport, build effective communication, and resolve conflicts. It is through such interaction that we determine whether others are worthy of our trust. There is neither a shortcut to trust nor a quick fix to its absence or violation.

I've worked with many organizations infected by what I call *systemic mistrust*, a pervasive climate of suspicion and defensiveness. The infection can be so severe that it becomes embedded at the meta-level, that is, people simply accept that "this is the way it is and the way it always will be." There's only one cure for systemic mistrust: openness and honesty. OD practitioners can play a crucial role in helping organizations create conditions favorable to openness and honesty by relying on the profession's rich body of concepts and tools, many of which have been developed by the other voices you have heard from in this chapter.

Peter Koestenbaum

I believe "9/11" was an OD event, and I see three OD needs and trends as a result:

1. *Deepening the Wisdom.* Deepening the insights and practices of OD is recognizing how the many issues confronted are not only topical but have their roots in the very nature of the human condition. We are biologically, psychologically, and socially well-equipped to grow by adapting to these dilemmas. To make that connection is the role of deepening.

   For example, how do we best motivate people? We can provide rewards and engineer an empowering environment. But it is still a superficial approach to this foundational requirement. We could instead challenge people about free will, freedom, and responsibility, and thus convey that motivation is a choice human beings make about who they are and what it means to be a person in the first place; what it means to work; and what it means to be a member of an organization. By deepening the understanding of the "stuck point," we can see anything that claims to be a solution or an adaptive transformation and watch it percolate up to the visible surface.

2. *Application to Strategy.* The suggestion here is that the future of OD lies in ever-increasing realism, ever-stronger contact with business objectives, and the harshness of business competition. This means knowing how to tolerate a hard world and how to be rugged oneself if necessary. It is to increase one's worth in realizing business objectives and to have the capacity to think in terms of "grand strategy."

   Grand strategy is approached through a simple and effective methodology: take any major news and then ask, "How did this situation develop historically? What have been the movements of peoples and of cultures, the clashes of nations and civilizations, the confrontations of ethnicities, the creation of artificial states by conquering armies, and how do these independent tributaries of history flow into the turbulent river of today's politics?" This gives you practice in thinking big, rehearsing grand strategy as a way of honing your OD skills. And then ask, "What do these grand strategy insights teach you about managing your business today?" The larger issues of the world are but the magnification of our daily and local business concerns. Actions always occur by working through others and with others. In other words, everything we accomplish is co-created, whether we wish it or not.

3. *Systematizing Theory and Foundations.* Kurt Lewin was fond of saying that there is nothing more practical than a good theory. A good theory provides a solid foundation. It gives credibility and legitimacy to praxis. A model and a theory compress millennia of experience in one condensed image. A verified theory supports the sanctity of truth against the onslaught of fantasy and speculation. OD is known for solid theory, and there is not much new coming forth, as my friend Bob Tannenbaum said. Such is the role of OD in establishing a philosophical foundation, not for theology and physics, but for OD's journey toward meaning in organizations.

   Depth, strategy, and theory—therein lie the future of organization development. This is 9/11 coming full circle—to become a fully mature profession worthy of its noble calling.

Peter Vaill

I have known Bob Tannenbaum since 1964. He was always able to establish a real relationship with whomever he was talking to—CEO, grad student, worker, faculty colleague—and to caringly and consistently communicate his vision of things within that actual relationship and to be respectful of the other person's vision of things, too. He was interested in what could grow out of the relationship, rather than in importing into it a whole load of ideas and aspirations that probably would not fit very well and only serve to make it harder for the parties to experience each other concretely.

I think OD has lost that aspect of itself. Many of the early founders were men and women who got up close and personal with their clients, their students, and their colleagues. Their visions of change were more concrete than is present in all of our contemporary verbiage. They had specific organizations in mind most of the time, with fairly specific kinds of challenges, and clients with fairly specific capacities to act. They kept talking about what could be accomplished within the current client relationships that they had. At least that's the way I experienced them.

I don't know if those in OD are supposed to save the world. I think a more sound and healthy strategy is to not lose ourselves in a maze of ungrounded concepts, but instead to work as fully and energetically as we can with those we encounter, with a vision of human potential, to make the changes that we can with them and the organizations they inhabit, knowing full well that the work is never going to be done, but if we don't do it, no one else will either.

Meg Wheatley

Thanks for that, Peter. I do feel we need to act from a place of consciousness. We've now learned enough about the way life works and we've learned a lot about the human spirit. I so want all those who are interested to be very anxiously engaged and thinking through how we look at new forms that actually honor, nourish, and sustain. I want to put my love behind preparing individuals to survive with their spirits intact. I want to make sure that people's lives are not destroyed. My ultimate message that I give now to others is to do what stirs your heart. That's where you'll find the courage to work on it. And as you're doing what really moves you, make sure you connect to others, because that's where the real power for exponential change is.

Sandra Janoff

I believe that we have a future only if we (individuals, groups, or nations) can make the developmental leap from "me at the center " to "me as a part of the whole." I remember when I was in Delhi, India, driving in a mini-van. We were on a large boulevard and I soon realized that there were no painted lanes, no order to the traffic flow, and the road was filled with cars, trucks, bikes, motorcycles, buses, walkers, goats, cows, and water buffalo. It was total chaos. I couldn't make sense of it. How could people put up with this?

And then I got it—there is another reality here. No one "owns" the road, no one sits at the center of that universe. The road is shared by whomever and whatever can use it as a path—each one is a part of a whole. This is far different from the experience I had in Boulder, Colorado, where traffic and "the right to the road" is one of the key tensions in their community. I worked with the community there to develop a new transportation plan. The bikers came ready to scapegoat the drivers, and the drivers came ready to scapegoat the bikers. They struggled with common ground, even though they acknowledged the irony in the fact that bikers also drove cars and the drivers also rode bikes. They have since developed a mutually agreed-on transportation plan, which should lessen the tension and support a shared picture.

Final Thoughts
Paula Griffin and Kristine Quade

We cannot predict the future. Its possibilities counsel us to be cautious, dare us to be bold, and give us great hope. Bob Tannenbaum reminded us that we have the power to change the world. Meg Wheatley asks us to do what stirs our hearts.

All the participants in this conversation have given us a lot to consider. From engaging our thoughts about the identity of the field and our purpose for being in it, through discussions of our principles, the models, methods, and tools we use, to the broadening of our perspective to include the whole world, and finally considering the future, it's been a wonderful visit with our colleagues.

In some ways, we've felt as though we were in the room with the participants in this conversation—moving from group to group, hearing people we've known for years and others we just met discuss the things that matter most to them and challenging our own thinking about what matters most to us.

As we opened this conversation, we likened it to the river, where we dip our bucket, taking what we need in the moment with the knowledge that the river will flow on. As you have nourished yourselves by the river, we hope you will share its gifts, and yours, by continuing the conversation.

We hope that you will convene some aspects of this conversation around whatever topics excite you or have meaning for you. As long as we remain creative, curious, searching for connections beyond the imagination, this field will continue to evolve and thrive. But before we go, we offer you a few last questions to consider, questions we hope will allow you to reflect on what has been shared here and to decide how you want to use it to shape your life, your practice, your world.

• FREEZE FRAME

As you go forth to get on with your OD practice, ask yourself these questions:

1. On reflection, what do I want to stand for as I interact with my clients? What is the centrality of my practice?

2. What has meaning for me that I will focus my attention on? How will I do that?

3. How would I describe the field of OD now? How is that different from what I would have said before reading this book?

4. What are my responsibilities to the global society and what does that mean to my practice?

5. What research or reading would I like to do on topics that were discussed here?

6. In what ways will I commit to furthering the conversation?

Bibliography

Ackerman Anderson, L., & Anderson, D. (2001). *Beyond change management: Advanced strategies for today's transformational leaders.* San Francisco, CA: Pfeiffer.

Adams, J.D. (1974). *Organization development and change.* Washington, DC: National Training and Development Service.

Adams, J.D. (1974). *Theory and method in organization development: An evolutionary process.* Arlington, VA: NTL Institute for Applied Behavioral Science.

Adams, J.D. (1989). *Understanding and managing stress: Instruments to assess your lifestyle.* San Francisco, CA: Pfeiffer.

Adams, J.D. (1998). *Transforming work.* Alexandria, VA: Miles River Press.

Allen, R.C. (2002). *Guiding change journeys: A synergistic approach to organization transformation.* San Francisco, CA: Pfeiffer.

Anderson, D., & Ackerman Anderson, L. (2001). *A roadmap for conscious transformation: Navigating organization change.* San Francisco, CA: Pfeiffer.

Axelrod, R.H. (2000). *Terms of engagement: Changing the way we change organizations.* San Francisco, CA: Berrett-Koehler.

Beck, D., & Cowan, C. (1996). *Mastering values, leadership, and change: Exploring the new science of memetics.* Cambridge, MA: Blackwell Business.

Beckhard, R., & Harris, R., (1987). *Organizational transitions.* Reading, MA: Addison-Wesley.

Beckhard, R., & Harris, R. (1992). *Changing the essence: The art of creating and leading fundamental change in organizations.* San Francisco, CA: Jossey-Bass.

Bellman, G.M. (1992). *Getting things done when you are not in charge.* San Francisco, CA: Berrett-Koehler.

Bellman, G.M. (2001). *The consultant's calling: Bringing who you are to what you do* (rev. ed.). San Francisco, CA: Jossey-Bass.

Block, P. (1999). *Flawless consulting: A guide to getting your expertise used* (2nd ed.). San Francisco, CA: Pfeiffer.

Bohm, D., & Nichol, L. (1996). *On dialogue.* New York: Rowthedge.

Bolman, L.G., & Deal, T.E. (1995). *Leading with soul: An uncommon journey of spirit.* San Francisco, CA: Jossey-Bass.

Bunker, B.B., & Alban, B.T. (1996). *Large group interventions: Engaging the whole system for rapid change.* San Francisco, CA: Jossey-Bass.

Burke, W. (1977). *Current issues and strategies in organization development.* New York: Human Sciences Press.

Burke, W. (1982). *Organization development: Principles and practices.* Glenview, IL: Scott, Foresman.

Burke, W. (1987). *Organization development: A normative view.* Reading, MA: Addison-Wesley.

Burke, W.W. (1990). *Leadership report.* Pelham, NY: W.W. Burke Associates.

Burke, W.W. (1994). *Organization development: A process of learning and changing.* Reading, MA: Addison-Wesley.

Burke, W.W., & Hornstein, H. (1972). *The social technology of organization development.* San Francisco, CA: Pfeiffer.

Burke, W.W., & Trahant, W. (2000). *Business climate shifts profiles of change makers.* Boston, MA: Butterworth Heinemann.

Byrd, J., & Brown, P. (2003). *The innovation equation: Building creativity and risk taking in your organization.* San Francisco, CA: Pfeiffer.

Carter, L., Giber, D., & Goldsmith, M. (Eds.). (2001). *Best practices in organization development and change.* San Francisco, CA: Pfeiffer/Linkage.

Coghlan, D. (1993). *Planned change in the Irish province of the Society of Jesus.* Dublin, Ireland: University College Dublin.

Cooperrider, D., Sorenson, P., Whitney, D., & Yaeger, T. (2000). *Appreciative inquiry: Rethinking human organization toward a positive theory of change.* Champaign, IL: Stipes.

Cooperrider, D., & Whitney, D.K. (1999). *Appreciative inquiry.* San Francisco, CA: Berrett-Koehler.

Cummings, T.G., & Worley, C. (2001). *Essentials of organization development and change.* Cincinnati, OH: South-Western.

Cummings, T.G., & Worley, C. (2001). *Organization development and change.* Cincinnati, OH: South-Western.

Dannemiller, K. (1999). *Whole-scale change.* San Francisco, CA: Berrett-Koehler.

Davis, S., Shephard, H., & Burke, W. (1980). *The pairing of internal and external OD consultants.* Los Angeles, CA: CREDR Corp.

Eoyang, G. (1997). *Coping with chaos: Seven simple tools,* Cheyenne, WY: Lagumo Corp.

Fischer, R., & Ury, W. (1991). *Getting to yes: Negotiating agreement without giving in.* New York: Penguin Books.

Golembiewski, R., Harvey, J., & Shivastva, S. (1980). *Technique or values: An emerging controversy among OD practitioners.* Los Angeles, CA: CREDR Corp.

Haass, R. (1994). *The power to persuade.* Boston, MA: Houghton Mifflin.

Hammond, S.A., & Royal, C. (1998). *Lessons from the field: Applying appreciative inquiry.* Plano, TX: Thin Book Publishing Co.

Hersey, P., & Blanchard K. (1969). *Management of organizational behavior.* Englewood Cliffs, NJ: Prentice Hall.

Jacobs, R. (1994). *Real time strategic change: How to involve an entire organization in fast and far-reaching change.* San Francisco, CA: Berrett-Koehler.

Jamieson, D., & O'Mara, J. (1991). *Managing workforce 2000: Gaining the diversity advantage.* San Francisco, CA: Jossey-Bass.

Justice, T., & Jamieson, D. (1999). *The facilitator's fieldbook: Step-by-step procedures, checklists and guidelines, samples and templates.* New York: AMACOM.

Karp, H., Fuller, C., & Sirias, D. (2002). *Bridging the boomer-Xer gap: Creating authentic teams for high performance at work.* Palo Alto, CA: Davies-Black.

Katz, J. (1978). *White awareness: Handbook for anti-racism training.* Norman, OK: University of Oklahoma Press.

Koestenbaum, P. (1991). *Leadership: The inner side of greatness.* San Francisco, CA: Jossey-Bass.

Koestenbaum, P., & Block, P. (2001). *Freedom and accountability at work: Applying philosophical insight to the real world.* San Francisco, CA: Pfeiffer.

Lewin, K. (1951). *Field theory in social science.* New York: Harper & Row.

Likert, R. (1967). *The human organization: Its management and value.* New York: McGraw-Hill.

Mabee, B. (2000, July/August). The four postures of influence. *Training Today.*

Mabee, B. (2000, September/October). The powers of three: Practical business diagnosis whether or not they ask. *Training Today.*

Mabee, B. (2000, November/December). Quick loops/rapid evolution. Two paths under pressure: Lack of time or loops of time? *Training Today.*

Markland, R.E., Vickery, S.K., & Davis, R. (1998). *Operations management: Concepts in manufacturing and services.* Cincinnati, OH: South-Western.

McWhinney, W., & Hutchison, K. (1992). *Paths of change: Strategic choices for organizations and society.* Thousand Oaks, CA: Sage.

Miller, F., & Katz, J. (2002). *The inclusion breakthrough: Unleashing the real power of diversity.* San Francisco, CA: Berrett-Koehler.

Mintzberg, H. (1983). *Structure in fives: Designing effective organizations.* Englewood Cliffs, NJ: Prentice Hall.

Mintzberg, H. (1994). *The rise and fall of strategic planning: Reconceiving roles for planning, plans, planners.* New York: The Free Press.

Mintzberg, H., & Ahlstrand, B.W. (1998). *Strategy safari: A guided tour through the wilds of strategic management.* New York: The Free Press.

Olson, E., & Eoyang, G. (2001). *Facilitating organization change: Lessons from complexity science.* San Francisco, CA: Pfeiffer.

Oshry, B. (1995). *Seeing systems: Unlocking the mysteries of organizational life.* San Francisco, CA: Berrett-Koehler.

Pfeiffer, J.W., & Jones, J.C. (1972–1981). *The annual handbook for group facilitators.* San Francisco, CA: Pfeiffer.

Pinault, L. (2000). *Consulting demons: Inside the unscrupulous world of global corporate consulting.* New York: Harper Business.

Quade, K., & Brown, R. (2002). *The conscious consultant: Mastering change from the inside out.* San Francisco, CA: Pfeiffer.

Schein, E.H. (1998). *Process consultation: Its role in organization development.* Reading, MA: Addison-Wesley.

Scott, B. (2000). *Consulting on the inside: An internal consultant's guide to living and working inside organizations.* Alexandria, VA: American Society for Training & Development.

Senge, P.M., Kleiner, A., Roberts, C., Ross, R.B., & Smith, B.J. (1994). *The fifth discipline fieldbook: Strategies and tools for building a learning organization.* New York: Doubleday Dell.

Sibbett, D. (1990). *Leading business teams: Groupware users' project.* Menlo Park, CA: Institute for the Future/San Francisco, CA: Graphic Guides, Inc.

Sorenson, P. (1991). *International organization development.* Champaign, IL: Stipes.

Sorenson, P., & Baum, B. (1974). *Perspectives on organizational behavior: An introduction and overview.* Champaign, IL: Stipes.

Spencer, S.A., & Adams, J.D. (1990). *Life changes: Growing through personal transitions.* San Luis Obispo, CA: Impact.

Tannenbaum, R.T., & Margulies, F. (1985). *Human systems development.* San Francisco, CA: Jossey-Bass.

Tannenbaum, R.T., Weschler, I.R., & Massarik, F. (1987). *Leadership and organization: A behavioral science approach.* New York: Garland.

Weisbord, M. (1976). Organizational diagnosis: Six places to look for trouble with or without a theory. *Group & Organization Studies, 1,* 430–447.

Weisbord, M. (1978). *Organizational diagnosis: A workbook of theory and practice.* Reading, MA: Addison-Wesley.

Weisbord, M. (1993). *Discovering common ground: How future search conferences bring people together to achieve breakthrough innovation, empowerment, shared vision, and collaborative action.* San Francisco, CA: Berrett-Koehler.

Weisbord, M., & Janoff, S. (1995). *Future search: An action guide to finding common ground in organizations and communities.* San Francisco, CA: Berrett-Koehler.

Wheatley, M. (1992). *Leadership and the new science: Learning about organization from an orderly universe.* San Francisco, CA: Berrett-Koehler.

Wheatley, M., (1997). *Self-organizing system: Creating the capacity for continuous change.* Cambridge, MA: Pegasus.

Wheatley, M. (1999). *Leadership and the new science: Discovering order in a chaotic world.* San Francisco, CA: Berrett-Koehler.

Wheatley, M. (2001). Voices: A poetic journey laced in humanity and celebrating village life from *Smarden: A wealden tapestry.* New York: Harmony.

Wheatley, M. (2002). *Turning to one another: Simple conversations to restore hope to the future.* San Francisco, CA: Berrett-Koehler.

Wheatley, M., & Kellner-Rogers, M. (1996). *A simpler way.* San Francisco, CA: Berrett-Koehler.

Wheatley, M., & Kellner-Rogers, M. (1997). *Natural creativity for organizations.* Ukiah, CA: New Dimensions Foundation.

Whitney, D.K. (2002). *Encyclopedia of positive questions, volume one: Using appreciative inquiry to bring out the best in your organization.* Euclid, OH: Lakeshore Communications.

Whitney, D.K., & Trosten-Bloom, A. (2003). *The power of appreciative inquiry: A practical guide to positive change.* San Francisco, CA: Berrett-Koehler.

Worley, C.G., Hitchin, D., & Ross, W. (1996). *Integrated strategic change: How OD builds competitive advantage.* Reading, MA: Addison-Wesley.

About the Series

THERE ARE WATERSHED MOMENTS in history that change everything after them. The attack on Pearl Harbor was one of those. The bombing of Hiroshima was another. The terrorist attack on the World Trade Center in New York City was our most recent. All resulted in significant change that transformed many lives and organizations.

Practicing Organization Development: The Change Agent Series for Groups and Organizations was launched to help those who must cope with or create change. The series is designed to share what is working or not working, to provoke critical thinking about change, and to offer creative ways to deal with change, rather than the destructive ones noted above.

The Current State of Change Management and Organization Development

Almost as soon as the ink was dry on the first wave of books published in this series, we heard that its focus was too narrow. We heard that the need for theory and practice extended beyond OD into change management. More than one respected authority urged us to reconsider our focus, moving beyond OD to include books on change management generally.

Organization development is not the only way that change can be engineered or coped with in organizational settings. We always knew that, of course. And we remain grounded in the view that change management, however it is carried out, should be based on such values as respect for the individual, participation and involvement in change by those affected by it, and interest in the improvement of organizational settings on many levels—including productivity improvement, but also improvement in achieving work/life balance and in a values-based approach to management and to change.

A Brief History of the Genesis of the Series

A few years ago, and as a direct result of the success of *Practicing Organization Development: A Guide for Practitioners* by Rothwell, Sullivan, and McLean, the publisher—feeling that OD was experiencing a rebirth of interest in the United States and in other nations—wanted to launch a new OD series. The goal of this new series was not to replace, or even compete directly with, the well-established Addison-Wesley OD Series (edited by Edgar Schein). Instead, as the editors saw it, the series would provide a means by which the most promising authors in OD whose voices had not previously been heard could share their ideas. The publisher enlisted the support of Bill Rothwell, Roland Sullivan, and Kristine Quade to turn the dream of a series into a reality.

This series was long in the making and has been steadily evolving since its inception. The original vision was an ambitious one—and involved no less than reinventing OD and re-energizing interest in the research and practice surrounding it. Sponsoring books was one means to that end. Another is the series website (www.pfeiffer.com/go/od). Far more than just a place to advertise the series, it serves as a real-time learning community for OD practitioners.

What Distinguishes the Books in this Series

The books in this series are meant to be challenging, cutting-edge, and state-of-the-art in their approach to OD and change management. The goal of the series is to provide an outlet for proven authorities in OD and change management who have not put their ideas into print or for up-and-coming writers in OD and change management who have new, sometimes unorthodox, approaches that are stimulating and exciting. Some books in this series describe inspirational concepts that can lead to actionable change and purvey ideas so new that they are not fully developed.

Unique to this series is the cutting-edge emphasis, the immediate applicability, and the ease of transferability of the concepts. The aim of this series is nothing less than to reinvent, re-energize, and reinvigorate OD and change management. In each book, we have also recommended that the author(s) provide:

- A research base of some kind, meaning new information derived from practice and/or systematic investigation and

- Practical tools, worksheets, case studies, and other ready-to-go approaches that help the authors drag "theory" to "practice" to make these new, cutting-edge approaches more concrete.

Subject Matter That Will (and Will Not) Be Covered

The books in this series are varied in their approach, but they are united by their focus. All share an emphasis on organization development (OD) and change management (CM). Hence, books in this series are about participative change efforts. They are not about such other popular topics as leadership, management development, consulting, or group dynamics—unless those topics are treated in new, cutting-edge ways and are geared to OD and change management practitioners.

This Book

Nearly one hundred organization development practitioners, from founders and leaders of the field to new graduates, participated in an online conversation covering all aspects of the field of OD. Launched by a discussion between Meg Wheatley and the late Bob Tannenbaum, the conversation challenges the field to consider its reasons for being, its methods of work, and its future. The resulting commentary has been organized into the five chapters of this book. In the first chapter, conversation participants explore matters of the identity and boundaries of the field of OD. Who are we? Why are we here? Whom do we serve? The second chapter concerns the critical questions around the principles and values of this "values-based" profession. In Chapter 3, practitioners describe the models and methods they use for their work—the ones they have invented themselves and the changes they have made to traditional models and methods taught in graduate programs. Chapter 4 brings the global perspective—examining the variables in global practice of an essentially Western field. In Chapter 5, senior practitioners and others consider the future of the field and the changes that must be made if it is to remain relevant and fulfill its promise. Like a friend or mentor describing his or her learning from years of experience, participants share stories, models, theories, beliefs, and helpful hints, making this book an important addition to any OD practitioner's library.

William J. Rothwell
University Park, PA

Roland Sullivan
Deephaven, MN

Kristine Quade
Minnetonka, MN

Statement
of the Board

IT IS OUR PLEASURE TO PARTICIPATE in and influence the start-up of *Practicing Organization Development: The Change Agent Series for Groups and Organizations*. The purpose of the series is to stimulate the profession and influence how organization change is defined and practiced. This statement is intended to set the context for the series by addressing three important questions: (1) What are the key issues facing organization change and development in the 21st Century? (2) Where does—or should—OD fit in the field of organization change and development? and (3) What is the purpose of this series?

What Are the Key Issues Facing Organization Change and Development in the 21st Century?

One of the questions is the extent to which leaders can control forces or can only be reactive. Will globalization and external forces be so powerful that they will prevent organizations from being able to "stay ahead of the change curve"? And what will be the role of technology, especially information technology, in the change process? To what extent can it be a carrier of change (as well as a source of change)?

What will the relationship be between imposed change and collaborative change? Will the increased education of the workforce demand the latter, or will the requirement of having to make fundamental changes demand leadership that sets goals that participants would not willingly set on their own? And what is the relationship between these two forms of change?

Who will be the change agent? Is this a separate profession, or will that increasingly be the responsibility of the organization's leaders? If the latter, how does that change the role of the change professional?

What will be the role of values for change in the 21st Century? Will the key values be performance—efficiency and effectiveness? And what role will the humanistic values of more traditional OD play? Or will the growth of knowledge (and human competence) as an organization's core competence make this a moot point in that performance can only occur if one takes account of humanistic values?

What is the relationship between other fields and the area of change? Can any change process that is not closely linked with strategy be truly effective? Can change agents focus only on process, or do they need to be knowledgeable and actively involved in the organization's products/services and understand the market niche in which the organization operates?

Where Does—or Should—OD Fit in the Field of Organization Change and Development?

We offer the following definition of OD to stimulate debate:

> Organization development is a system-wide and values-based collaborative process of applying behavioral science knowledge to the adaptive development, improvement, and reinforcement of such organizational features as the strategies, structures, processes, people, and cultures that lead to organization effectiveness.

The definition suggests that OD can be understood in terms of its several foci:

First, *OD is a system-wide process.* It works with whole systems. In the past, the bias has been toward working at the individual and group levels. More recently, the focus has shifted to organizations and multi-organization systems. We support that trend in general, but honor and acknowledge the fact that the traditional focus on smaller systems is both legitimate and necessary.

Second, *OD is values-based.* Traditionally, OD has attempted to distinguish itself from other forms of planned change and applied behavioral science by promoting a set of humanistic values and by emphasizing the importance of personal growth as a key to its practice. Today, that focus is blurred and there is much debate about the value base underlying the practice of OD. We support a more formal and direct conversation about what these values are and how the field is related to them.

Third, *OD is collaborative.* Our first value commitment as OD practitioners is to bring about an inclusive, diverse workforce with a focus of integrating differences into a world-wide culture mentality.

Fourth, *OD is based on behavioral science knowledge.* Organization development should incorporate and apply knowledge from sociology, psychology, anthropology, technology, and economics toward the end of making systems more effective. We support the continued emphasis in OD on behavioral science knowledge and believe that OD practitioners should be widely read and comfortable with several of the disciplines.

Fifth, *OD is concerned with the adaptive development, improvement, and reinforcement of strategies, structures, processes, people, culture, and other features of organizational life.* This statement describes not only the organizational elements that are the target of change but also the process by which effectiveness is increased. That is, OD works in a variety of areas, and it is focused on improving those areas. We believe that such a statement of process and content strongly implies that a key feature of OD is the transference of knowledge and skill to the system so that it is more able to handle and manage change in the future.

Sixth and finally, *OD is about improving organization effectiveness.* It is not just about making people happy; it is also concerned with meeting financial goals, improving productivity, and addressing stakeholder satisfaction. We believe that OD's future is closely tied to the incorporation of this value in its purpose and the demonstration of this objective in its practice.

This definition raises a host of questions:

- Are OD and organization change and development one and the same, or are they different?

- Has OD become just a collection of tools, methods, and techniques? Has it lost its values?

- Does it talk "systems," but ignore them in practice?

- Are consultants facilitators of change or activists of change?

- To what extent should consulting be driven by consultant value versus holding only the value of increasing the client's effectiveness?

- How can OD practitioners help formulate strategy, shape the strategy development process, contribute to the content of strategy, and drive how strategy will be implemented?

- How can OD focus on the drivers of change external to individuals, such as the external environment, business strategy, organization change, and culture change, as well as on the drivers of change internal to individuals, such as individual interpretations of culture, behavior, style, and mindset?

- How much should OD be part of the competencies of all leaders? How much should it be the sole domain of professionally trained, career-oriented OD practitioners?

What Is the Purpose of This Series?

This series is intended to provide current thinking about organization change and development as a field and to provide practical approaches based on sound theory and research. It is targeted for full-time external or internal change practitioners; top executives in charge of enterprise-wide change; and managers, HR practitioners, training and development professionals, and others who have responsibility for change in organizational and trans-organizational settings. At the same time, these books will be directed toward cutting-edge thinking and state-of-the-art approaches. In some cases, the ideas, approaches, or techniques described are still evolving, so the books are intended to open up dialogue.

We know that the books in this series will provide a leading forum for thought-provoking dialogue within the field.

About the Board Members

David Bradford is senior lecturer in organizational behavior at the Graduate School of Business, Stanford University, Palo Alto, California. He is co-author (with Allan R. Cohen) of *Managing for Excellence, Influence Without Authority,* and *POWER UP: Transforming Organizations Through Shared Leadership.*

W. Warner Burke is professor of psychology and education in the department of organization and leadership at Teachers College at Columbia University in New York. He also serves as a senior advisor to PricewaterhouseCoopers. His most recent publication is *Business Profiles of Climate Shifts: Profiles of Change Makers,* with William Trahant and Richard Koonce.

Edith Whitfield Seashore is an organization consultant and co-founder (with Morley Segal) of AUNTL Masters Program in Organization Development. She is co-author of *What Did You Say?* and *The Art of Giving and Receiving Feedback* and co-editor of *The Promise of Diversity.*

Robert Tannenbaum was emeritus professor of development of human systems, Graduate School of Management, University of California, Los Angeles, and recipient of the Lifetime Achievement Award by the National OD Network. He published numerous books, including *Human Systems Development* (with Newton Margulies and Fred Massarik).

Christopher G. Worley is director, MSOD Program, Pepperdine University, Malibu, California. He is co-author of *Organization Development and Change* (7th ed.), with Tom Cummings, and of *Integrated Strategic Change,* with David Hitchin and Walter Ross.

Shaolin Zhang is senior manager of organization development for Motorola (China) Electronics Ltd. He received his master's degree in American Studies from Beijing Foreign Studies University, Beijing, China, and holds a Ph.D. in sociology from York University, Toronto, Ontario.

Afterword
to the Series

ON **1967,** Warren Bennis, Ed Schein, and I were faculty members of the Sloan School of Management at MIT. We decided to produce a series of paperback books that collectively would describe the state of the field of organization development (OD). Organization development as a field had been named by me and several others from our pioneer change effort at General Mills in Minneapolis, Minnesota, some ten years earlier.

Today I define OD as "a systemic and systematic change effort, using behavioral science knowledge and skill, to transform the organization to a new state."

In any case, several books and many articles had been written, but there was no consensus on whether OD was a field of practice, an area of study, or a profession. We had not even established OD as a theory or even as a practice.

We decided that there was a need for something that would describe the state of OD. Our intention was to each write a book and also to recruit three other authors. After some searching, we found a young editor who had just joined the small publishing house of Addison-Wesley. We made contact, and the series was born. Our audience was to be human resource professionals who spent their time consulting with managers in their development through various small-group activities, such as team building. More than thirty books have been published in that series, and the series has had a life of its own. We just celebrated its thirtieth anniversary.

At last year's National OD Network Conference, I said that it was time for the OD profession to change and transform itself. Is that not what we change agents tell our clients to do? This new Jossey-Bass/Pfeiffer series will do just that. It can be seen as:

- A documentation of the re-invention of OD;

- An effort that will take us to the next level; and

- A practical effort to transfer to the world the theory and practice of leading-edge practitioners and theorists.

The books in this new series will thus prove to be valuable resources for change agents to keep current with the new and leading-edge ideas and practices.

May this very exciting change agent series be most creative and innovative. May it give our field a renewed burst of energy and awareness.

Richard Beckhard
Written on Labor Day weekend 1999 from my summer cabin near Bethel, Maine

About the Series Editors

William J. Rothwell, Ph.D., is president of Rothwell and Associates, a private consulting firm, as well as professor of human resources development on the University Park Campus of The Pennsylvania State University. Before arriving at Penn State in 1993, he was an assistant vice president and management development director for a major insurance company and a training director in a state government agency. He has worked full-time in human resources management and employee training and development from 1979 to the present. He thus combines real-world experience with academic and consulting experience. As a consultant, Dr. Rothwell's client list includes over thirty-five companies from the Fortune 500.

Dr. Rothwell received his Ph.D. with a specialization in employee training from the University of Illinois at Urbana-Champaign, his M.B.A. with a specialization in human resources management from Sangamon State University (now called the

University of Illinois at Springfield), his M.A. from the University of Illinois at Urbana-Champaign, and his B.A. from Illinois State University. He holds lifetime accreditation as a Senior Professional in Human Resources (SPHR), has been accredited as a Registered Organization Development Consultant (RODC), and holds the industry designation as Fellow of the Life Management Institute (FLMI).

Dr. Rothwell's latest publications include *The Manager and Change Leader* (ASTD, 2001); *The Role of Intervention Selector, Designer and Developer, and Implementor* (ASTD, 2000); *ASTD Models for Human Performance* (2nd ed.) (ASTD, 2000); *The Analyst* (ASTD, 2000); *The Evaluator* (ASTD, 2000); *The ASTD Reference Guide to Workplace Learning and Performance* (3rd ed.), with H. Sredl (HRD Press, 2000); *The Complete Guide to Training Delivery: A Competency-Based Approach,* with S. King and M. King (AMACOM, 2000); *Human Performance Improvement: Building Practitioner Competence,* with C. Hohne and S. King (Butterworth-Heinemann, 2000); *Effective Succession Planning: Ensuring Leadership Continuity and Building Talent from Within* (2nd ed.) (AMACOM, 2000); and *The Competency Toolkit,* with D. Dubois (HRD Press, 2000).

Roland Sullivan, RODC, has worked as an OD pioneer with nearly eight hundred systems in eleven countries and virtually every major industry. Richard Beckhard has recognized him as one of the world's first one hundred change agents.

Mr. Sullivan specializes in the science and art of systematic and systemic change, executive team building, and facilitating Whole System Transformation Conferences—large interactive meetings with 300 to 1,500 people. Over 25,000 people have participated in his conferences worldwide; one co-facilitated with Kristine Quade held for the Amalgamated Bank of South Africa was named runner-up for the title of outstanding change project of the world by the OD Institute.

With William Rothwell and Gary McLean, he is revising one of the field's seminal books, *Practicing OD: A Consultant's Guide* (Jossey-Bass/Pfeiffer, 1995). The first edition is now translated into Chinese.

He did his graduate work in organization development at Pepperdine University and Loyola University.

Mr. Sullivan's current interests include the following: Whole-system transformation, balancing economic and human realities; discovering and collaborating with cutting-edge change-focused authors who are documenting the perpetual renewal of the OD profession; and applied phenomenology: developing higher states of consciousness and self-awareness in the consulting of interdependent organizations.

Mr. Sullivan's current professional learning is available at www.rolandsullivan.com.

Kristine Quade is an independent consultant who combines her background as an attorney with a master's degree in organization development from Pepperdine University and years of experience as both an internal and external OD consultant.

Ms. Quade draws from experiences in guiding teams from divergent areas within corporations and across many levels of executives and employees. She has facilitated leadership alignment, culture change, support system alignment, quality process improvements, organizational redesign, and the creation of clear strategic intent that results in significant bottom-line results. A believer in whole-system change, she has developed the expertise to facilitate groups ranging in size from eight to two thousand in the same room for a three-day change process.

Recognized as the 1996 Minnesota Organization Development Practitioner of the Year, Ms. Quade teaches in the master's programs at Pepperdine University and the University of Minnesota at Mankato and the master's and doctoral programs at the University of St. Thomas in Minneapolis. She is a frequent presenter at the Organization Development National Conference and also at the International OD Congress and the International Association of Facilitators.

About the
Book Editors

Margaret Wheatley writes, teaches, and speaks about radically new practices and ideas for organizing in chaotic times. She works to create organizations of all types where people are known as the blessing, not the problem. She is president of The Berkana Institute, a charitable global foundation serving life-affirming leaders around the world, and has been an organizational consultant for many years, as well as a professor of management in two graduate programs. Her latest book, *Turning to One Another: Simple Conversations to Restore Hope to the Future* (2002), proposes that real social change comes from the ageless process of people thinking together in conversation. Ms. Wheatley's work also appears in two award-winning books, *Leadership and the New Science* (1992, 1999) and *A Simpler Way* (with Myron Kellner-Rogers, 1996), plus several videos and articles. She draws many of her ideas from new science and life's ability to organize in self-organizing, systemic, and cooperative modes. Increasingly, her models for new organizations are drawn from her understanding of many different cultures and spiritual traditions. Her articles and work can be accessed at www.margaretwheatley.com.

Robert **Tannenbaum** was one of the founders of the field of organization development. He was affiliated with such organizations as NTL Institute for Applied Behavioral Science, the University of California, and the Organization Development Network. He was emeritus professor of the development of human systems, Anderson Graduate School of Management, UCLA, and the recipient of the Lifetime Achievement Award from the National OD Network. He taught many students, co-edited two books, wrote for journals, and gave presentations to practitioners across the world. He passed away on March 14th, 2003.

Paula **Yardley Griffin** is a consultant, author, and editor. Following twenty years of consulting, training, and human resource management positions in financial service corporations in the New York area, she moved to external consulting, serving a range of clients from financial services to high-technology and not-for-profit organizations. Since 1997, along with consulting work, she has been the publisher/editor of *Consulting Today*, a newsletter for consultants, coaches, and facilitators. Her MSOD is from Pepperdine University. Now based in the Lehigh Valley of Eastern Pennsylvania, Ms. Griffin can be reached at pygriffin@aol.com.

Kristine **Quade** is an independent consultant and combines her background as an attorney with a master's degree in organization development from

Pepperdine University and over twenty years of experience as both an internal and external OD consultant. Recognized as the 1996 Minnesota Organization Development practitioner of the year, Ms. Quade also teaches in several master's and doctoral programs. Along with others, she self-published *The Essential Handbook: Behind the Scenes of Large Group Events* in 1996 and co-authored *The Conscious Consultant: Mastering Change from the Inside Out*, published by Pfeiffer in 2002. Ms. Quade serves as a board member for the National Organization Development Network and is a member of National Training Labs (NTL).

Organization Development Network (OD Network) is a vital learning community that develops, supports, and inspires practitioners and enhances the body of knowledge in human organization and systems development.

Members of the Organization Development Network are practitioners representing a range of professional roles in a wide variety of organizations. About half the members are employed by private industry, non-profit organizations, and government agencies. The other half operate their own consulting firms, engage in private practice, and/or teach.

The OD Network is the largest U.S.-based organization for organization development practitioners. While the majority of members are from North America, the association has members from countries around the world.

About the
Contributors

John Adams, Ph.D., has spent more than thirty years in the OD world, including a stint at NTL and twenty years of professional practice focusing on transitions, stress and health, vision and purpose, and sustainable development. Beginning in 1995, he worked internally at Sun Microsystems and then Blue Shield of California. These jobs helped him to reconnect and learn first-hand about the experience of work at the end of the 20th Century. In 1999, John joined the faculties of both Saybrook Graduate School and The Union Institute & University.

John G. Agno is president of Signature, Inc., an executive and business coaching firm located in Ann Arbor, Michigan. As a former corporate executive and management consultant, he understands that in the business world, people don't speak much about the heart and knows that people need a life full of connection, belonging, and meaningful contribution.

Billie T. Alban is president and senior partner of Alban and Williams, Ltd. Her consulting activities include strategic planning and organizational redesign. She has worked with joint ventures and helped in the development of international management teams. In recent years, her practice has been focused on working with organizations and communities on large-scale change efforts. She has been on the staff of the Tavistock Institute in England, has served as dean for the Presidents and Executives Workshops for the National Training Laboratories, and has been part of the core faculty for executive and management programs at Columbia University, UCLA, Pepperdine University, and others. She is on the board of advisors of the Yale Divinity School. Her most recent book, with Barbara Bunker, is *Large Group Interventions: Engaging the Whole System for Rapid Change.*

Glenn **P. Allen-Meyer** is a full-time consultant with the Kaleel Jamison Consulting Group, Inc., and author of the book entitled *Nameless Organizational Change.* Prior to joining KJCG, Mr. Allen was the manager of organization development for Epcot at Walt Disney World and senior internal organization development consultant at Cornell University. He can be reached at www.nameless.org.

Linda **Ackerman Anderson** is co-founder and vice president of Being First, Inc., a training and consulting firm specializing in leading conscious transformation in Fortune 1000 companies. She was one of the original creators of the field of organization transformation in the early 1980s and speaks on the topic around the world. She co-authored *The Change Leader's Roadmap: How to Navigate Your Organization's Transformation* and *Beyond Change Management: Advanced Strategies for Transformational Leaders* and spearheaded the development of the landmark Change Process Model for Leading Conscious Transformation. She coaches senior change leaders on their enterprise-wide change strategies and specializes in developing women as leaders of change.

Deborah **Arcoleo** is an OD/OE consultant in the New York/New Jersey metro area with over twenty years' experience in process consulting, program design, and facilitation to organizations of all sizes and in many industries. She has worked in the financial services industry and for several of the large consulting firms, including McKinsey & Company. She also ran a consulting practice for Lee Hecht Harrison, a leading outplacement provider. Ms. Arcoleo has a B.A. in economics from Indiana University and an M.A. in organization design and effectiveness from the Fielding Institute in Santa Barbara. Contact her at darcoleo @strategyquest.com.

Richard H. Axelrod is a founder of and principal in The Axelrod Group, Inc., a consulting firm that pioneered the use of employee involvement to effect large-scale organizational change through the use of the Conference Model, which he co-created with his wife Emily. His bachelor's degree is in industrial management from Purdue University, and his MBA is from the University of Chicago. Axelrod has served as adjunct faculty for Loyola University, Benedictine University, and the University of Chicago. He is the author of *Terms of Engagement: Changing the Way We Change Organizations* and a contributing author to *Discovering Common Ground, The Change Handbook,* and *The Flawless Consulting Field Book.*

Glenn R. Ayres is a national family business consultant working in a multidisciplinary environment to assist families in business together with such diverse tasks as ownership and management succession, professionalization of their management team, governance, wealth management, and education, and transitions in personal and professional careers. Ayres is the current president of The Family Firm Institute, an adjunct faculty member in the Business School of the University of St. Thomas, and a doctoral candidate in organization development.

Ann Bares has spent the last seventeen years consulting with a wide range of organizations in the areas of measuring, managing, and rewarding employee performance. She is a frequent speaker and instructor, currently teaching courses at the University of Minnesota and Concordia University. Bares received her MBA with a focus on organizational behavior from the J.L. Kellogg School of Management at Northwestern University in Evanston, Illinois. She can be contacted at annbares@earthlink.net.

Geoff Bellman, author and consultant, has worked with organizations for thirty years, writing five books along the way, including *The Consultant's Calling: Bringing Who You Are to What You Do.* His most recent book is *The Beauty of the Beast: Breathing New Life into Organizations.* He lives in Seattle and can be reached at Geoffbellman@yahoo.com.

Barbara Benedict Bunker is professor emerita of psychology at the University at Buffalo (SUNY). She also teaches in executive development programs at Columbia and Pepperdine Universities. She has been active as a consultant for over thirty years with clients both in the United States and abroad. Her books include *Large Group Interventions* (1997) with Billie Alban. She can be contacted at bbunker@buffalo.edu.

W. **Warner Burke** is the author of more than one hundred articles and book chapters on organization development, training, change and organizational psychology, and conference planning, and author, co-author, editor, and co-editor of fourteen books. His latest book is *Organization Change: Theory and Practice.* He teaches leadership, organizational dynamics and theory, and organization change and consultation at Teachers College, Columbia University, New York. For eight years, he was a full-time professional with NTL and has edited journals for the American Management Association and the Academy of Management. Burke has consulted with a variety of organizations in business-industry, education, government, religion, medical systems, and professional services firms. He is currently serving as senior advisor to the strategy and organization change practice of IBM Global Business Services.

Jacqueline Byrd, Ph.D., is president of the Richard Byrd Company, a forty-year-old Minneapolis-based management consulting firm that serves both national and international clients. Byrd has focused her life's work on understanding organizations and helping individuals within those organizations leverage their capacity for greater success. She is also the brain behind *Creatrix.* As an author and speaker, she has published on and addressed the subjects of innovation, leadership, team effectiveness, and strategies for implementing change. Her newest book is *The Innovation Equation.* She can be contacted through www.creatrix.com.

Steven H. Cady, Ph.D., is the director of the Master of Organization Development Program and former director of the Institute for Organizational Effectiveness at Bowling Green State University (BGSU). He is also the editor for the *Organization Development Journal,* the oldest premier practitioner scholar journal that publishes articles on organization development and change management. Prior to receiving his Ph.D. in organizational behavior with a support area in research methods and psychology from Florida State University, Cady studied at the University of Central Florida, where he obtained an MBA and a BSBA in finance. He is strongly committed to using cutting-edge approaches that inspire system-wide change in organizations and is actively pursuing research and practice that unleashes passion at the individual and organizational levels.

Ron A. Carucci is a partner with Mercer Delta Consulting, LLC, a management consulting firm that provides services related to the management of strategic organizational change to major corporations. He works in the areas of executive leadership, building executive teams, strategy formulation and implementation, organization architecture, and large-scale enterprise and culture change. Carucci is a faculty member at Fordham University Graduate School. He is co-author of the books, *The Value Creating Consultant: How to Build and Sustain Lasting Client Relationships* (2000) and *Relationships That Enable Enterprise Change: Leveraging the Client-Consultant Connection* (2002).

David Coghlan teaches at the University of Dublin, Ireland. His main areas of research and teaching are in OD and action research, particularly clinical inquiry and insider action research. He is the author of *Doing Action Research in Your Own Organization* (with Teresa Brannick; Sage, 2001); and another book on OD for the Irish health system, *Changing Healthcare Organisations*, with Eilish McAuliffe.

Kathleen D. Dannemiller is founder and partner emeritus of Dannemiller Tyson Associates and a passionate advocate for whole-system change for more than thirty years. She is a worldwide authority on the complexities of whole-systems change. She has written numerous articles and has taught many others around the world how to do these methodologies. She is a constant learner and is currently enrolled in Saybrook's doctoral program in organizational studies. Dannemiller can be reached by email at kathie@danemillertyson.com.

Karen J. Davis, a global organizational consultant for almost thirty years, is based in New York City. Her clients include private and public sectors, nongovernmental, and non-profit organizations nationally and internationally. She is on the faculty of the OD master's program at University Diego Portales in Chile. She is actively involved in ODN (Organization Development Network) and IODA (International Organization Development Association). She describes herself as a "global citizen and gardener."

Daphne DePorres, Ed.D., is a U.S. citizen living in Monterrey, Neuvo Leon, Mexico, serving as the director of the master's degree program in organization development at the Universidad de Monterrey. She can be reached at daphne_udem@yahoo.com.

Becky DeStefano, Ph.D., is president of Consulting Futures and Consulting-U.com. With almost twenty years of experience in OD consulting and training, DeStefano is currently spending her time building her central location for the training of consultants—Consulting-U.com.

Julie DiBenedetto is the founder and principal consultant of Building InterConnections, an OD firm dedicated to helping school districts and their stakeholders build effective learning communities. DiBenedetto has over fifteen years' experience with organization development and improvement strategies in partnership with large and small organizations in both the private and public sectors. She can be reached at BuildConnections@aol.com.

Francis (Frank) M. Duffy is a professor of education administration and supervision at Gallaudet University in Washington, D.C., where he teaches organization behavior, development, theory and design, diagnosis, and redesign. He has published four books on systemic school improvement.

Glenda Eoyang, Ph.D., is a student and teacher of human systems dynamics, the emerging field of study that explores intersections between complexity and the social sciences. She is executive director of the Human Systems Dynamics Institute, president of Chaos Limited, Inc., author of *Coping with Chaos: Seven Simple Tools* (1997), and co-author of *Facilitating Organization Change: Lessons from Complexity Science* (2001). She writes and consults internationally to help individuals and organizations leverage the dynamics of human systems to respond to real-world challenges and opportunities.

Patricia "Petey" Firestone is the director of organization development for the Los Angeles County Fire Department. She has over fifteen years of internal and external consulting experience in the field of OD. Her clients represent a wide variety of for-profit and non-profit organizations specializing in health care, retail and foodservice, international entertainment, and public safety.

William Gellermann, retired, is vice president and U.N. representative of the Communications Coordination Committee for the United Nations, one of the oldest NGOs. His Ph.D. is from UCLA's Graduate School of Management.

D. **Kirk Hamilton** is a founding principal of Watkins Hamilton Ross Architects of Houston. He recently launched the consulting division of the firm, Q Group Advisors, doing vision, strategy, and organization design consulting for healthcare organizations. With more than twenty-five years' experience in hospital design, he was the founding president of the American College of Healthcare Architects. He has authored numerous articles and several publications, including *Innovations in Planning for Healthcare* and *Unit 2000: Patient Beds for the Future*. Hamilton is completing his MSOD degree at Pepperdine University.

Ed **Hampton** is the principal of Performance Perspectives, LLC, a firm that provides organization development consulting, performance coaching, and leadership development, a faculty member of the industrial engineering and management systems department at the University of Central Florida, co-owner of Ovideo Florist, and a retired Army officer. He has an M.S. in systems management from the University of Southern California. He is also a graduate of the U.S. Army Organizational Effectiveness Center and School and the U.S. Air Force Command and Staff College.

Bill **Harris** is a consultant, facilitator, and writer. He is focused on helping people by helping the organizations in which they work and live be sustainably, ethically successful. He helps people address complex issues through simulation-based systems thinking, and he helps people work more effectively in groups, be they face-to-face or online. He can be reached at bill_harris@facilitatedsystems.com.

David **Hock Wang Heng,** MSOD, has held diverse managerial positions in the Singapore Police Force. He is currently the head of the Organisation Excellence Unit in the Singapore Economic Development Board. Recognized for his steadfast promotion of OD values and principles among business leaders and executives, Heng was asked to help found the Singapore OD Group and the Community of Practice for OD practitioners at the Singapore Training and Development Association. He earned his MSc in organization development from Pepperdine University.

Stan Herman has more than thirty years of experience as an internal manager (GE and TRW) and external consultant, working with senior and middle management of Fortune 200 (and some smaller) companies. His focus is on coaching and counseling executives, planning and implementing highly focused, situation-specific improvement efforts, and other organization issues related to networked and new economy work groups. He is the author of five books and has also written more than one hundred articles and columns published in professional journals, popular magazines, business press, and general newspapers. Two books have been adapted as videos. Most recently he has edited *Rewiring Organizations for the Networked Economy* (2003).

Ken Hultman is an independent organization development consultant. He is the author of *Making Change Irresistible: Overcoming Resistance to Change in Your Organization* and *Balancing Individual and Organizational Values: Walking the Tightrope to Success.* He can be contacted at www.kenhultman.com.

Robert (Jake) Jacobs cares deeply about freeing people and organizations to create their future, faster. His work focuses on how to make big changes happen fast—and sustain them over time. He has also contributed to the field of organization development by authoring *Real Time Strategic Change: How to Involve an Entire Organization in Fast and Far-Reaching Change* (1994, 1997) and contributing stories and insights from his practice to books like *The Conscious Consultant* (2002). He can be contacted at rwj@rwjacobs.com.

David W. Jamieson is president of the Jamieson Consulting Group and adjunct professor of management at Pepperdine University in the MSOD Program. He has over thirty years of experience consulting to organizations on change, strategy, design, and human resource issues. He serves on the editorial boards for the *Journal of Organization Change Management, Journal of Management Inquiry,* and *The Organization Development Practitioner.* Jamieson is co-author of *Managing Workforce 2000: Gaining the Diversity Advantage* (1991) and of *The Complete Guide to Facilitation: Enabling Groups to Succeed* (1998). Today he is focused on advancing our understanding of organization change and consultation.

Sandra Janoff, Ph.D., plans, designs, and facilitates whole-systems processes known as future search in the public and private sector. She and her partner, Marvin Weisbord, design events that get the whole system together focusing on the future and creating values-based action strategies. She is a founder and co-director of Future Search Network, a non-profit organization that provides future searches anywhere in the world for whatever people can afford. Janoff is co-author of *Future Search: An Action Guide to Finding Common Ground in Organizations and Communities* (2nd ed., 2000). She can be reached at fsn@futuresearch.net.

Mike Jay received his bachelor's degree from Texas A&M University. He is the author of *Coaching as a Transformational Leadership Competency*. He founded B\Coach, an executive coach training system.

Marti Kaplan has over twenty-five years' experience in the evolving field of OD, focusing mostly on emergent situations in organizations of all sizes. A recent passion is working with large groups as they find common ground and create their futures together. Kaplan lives in San Francisco and can be reached at martikap@sbcglobal.net.

Hank Karp is an OD consultant, university professor, author, and principal of Personal Growth Systems in Chesapeake, Virginia. Karp's work focuses on team building, conflict management, executive development, and employing the Gestalt approach to individual and organizational growth. He has published many articles and four books, his most recent being *Bridging the Boomer—Xer Gap*, which deals with generational conflict in the work setting. He can be contacted at pgshank@aol.com.

Judith Katz is the executive vice president of The Kaleel Jamison Consulting Group, Inc., specializing in integrating culture change initiatives into business strategies of organizations. She serves on the boards of directors for Social Venture Network and The Group for Cultural Documentation. She is also a member of the Diversity Collegium, a think tank of diversity professionals in the United States. Katz is the author of *White Awareness: Handbook for Anti-Racism Training* (1978) and co-author, with Frederick A. Miller, of *The Inclusion Breakthrough: Unleashing the Real Power of Diversity* (2002).

Roselyn Kay is president of New Heights Group, LLC, an organization/change management, executive coaching, and strategic planning organization. Prior to starting her own company, she was with Fannie Mae in Washington, D.C., and served in senior leadership roles with New England banking and mortgage banking entities. Her MSOD is from AUNTL, and she recently completed both the organization development certificate and leadership coaching certificate at Georgetown University.

Peter Koestenbaum, Ph.D., has been a leadership consultant for more than a generation, and his work has carried him to over forty countries. He is an author and an emeritus philosophy professor. Among his recent books is *The Philosophic Consultant.* You can reach him at Peter@PiB.net.

Aurelie T. Laurence, Ph.D., has over twenty-five years in human resources, organizational consulting, coaching, and training. Laurence specializes in leadership development and facilitating groups to achieve organizational change. She has taught at numerous colleges, including American University, University of Maryland, and Loyola University. She can be reached at aurelie@comcast.net.

Bruce Mabee has, for twenty-five years, applied strategic planning, group facilitation, and individual consultation to help organizations, their members, and their leaders reach their major goals. Mabee prefers long-term relationships that apply a wide variety of tools and creativity. His clients have included Motorola, The Federal Aviation Administration, small social service agencies, and creative enterprises. His master's degree in OD is from George Williams College. His services have been used in the United States, Europe, Asia, and Latin America. He can be reached at bmabee@aol.com.

Robert J. Marshak, Ph.D., is an organizational consultant, educator, and author. He has a global practice with over twenty-five years' experience helping organizations plan changes, develop new strategies and structures, challenge limiting mindsets, work cross-culturally, and build more effective teamwork. Marshak is the author of over two dozen articles and book chapters on consulting and changes, including several that are considered classics in the field. He is known internationally for his pioneering work on Confucian change philosophy, covert processes, and the use of metaphor and meaning in organizational diagnosis and intervention. He has also worked with thousands of participants in OD and change leadership programs at NTL Institute, American University, Johns Hopkins University, Georgetown University, the University of Texas at Dallas, King's College London, Korea University, and the Singapore Training and Development Association. Marshak was awarded the Organization Development Network's Lifetime Achievement Award in 2000.

Guadalupe **(Lupita) Martínez de León** is a senior external consultant in Mexico. She has master's degrees in both organization development and education with a specialty in adult learning and a bachelor's degree in business from the University of Monterrey, Mexico. She worked for twenty years at executive levels in manufacturing enterprises, banks, and corporatives, then as director and professor of the OD Master's Program at the University of Monterrey, Mexico. Martinez has worked in cultural and strategic changes, reengineering process, diagnosing the executive and organizational performance, facilitating more than fifty learning communities.

Thomas **C. Matera** is a partner in Highland Consulting, the originators of Conversation by Design™, a curriculum of learning and application that creates clarity of intent and resolution for the purpose of achieving transformational results.

Bob **McCarthy** is an advisor and coach to leaders and a consultant in the management of change. As founder and head of McCarthy and Company, Bob has worked with innovative leaders of business, labor, government, health care, and education building high-performance organizations that engage the talent and passion of people. Based in Portland, Oregon, Bob can be reached at rmccarthy@mccarthyconsultants.com.

Jeff **McCollum** has been involved in large-scale organizational change as a line manager, internal consultant, and external consultant for more than thirty years. Leadership development, as a theme, has played through all of this work. He is currently in transition from an internal role with Pfizer Consumer Healthcare, driven by a belief that an internal consultant has about a five-year "half life" at most. He holds an AB degree from Princeton, an MSOD degree from Pepperdine, and is a member of the board of trustees of the Greenleaf Center for Servant Leadership.

Anne Kohnke Meda is currently working on her Ph.D. in organization development at Benedictine University in Lisle, Illinois. She has spent the past eighteen years in the information technology field, specializing in large software development projects, designing and building LAN/WAN networks, and telecommunications. Her OD experience has been in managing specialized work groups, team building, and leadership development. Contact her at medaanne @comcast.net.

Frederick A. Miller has been president and CEO of The Kaleel Jamison Consulting Group, Inc., since 1985. He was the recipient of the 2000 Outstanding Service to the Organization Development Network Award and was noted in *The Age of Heretics* as one of the forerunners of corporate change. In addition to being a former board member of Ben & Jerry's Homemade, Inc., he has served on the boards of directors of National Training Labs, the OD Network, and American Society for Training and Development and as managing editor of *The Promise of Diversity* (1994). He is co-author, with Judith H. Katz, of *The Inclusion Breakthrough: Unleashing the Real Power of Diversity* (2002).

Matt Minahan received his doctorate from The George Washington University. He is president of MM & Associates, an international consulting firm specializing in strategic planning, organization design, and executive development for large, complex systems.

Michael Mitchell has over thirty years' experience as an OD practitioner. He has worked internally, founding the OD function for Kaiser Aluminum and Chemical Corporation; as an academic, teaching in the Pepperdine MSOD program, at San Francisco State, and Chico State in California; and as an external, working alone and in partnership with other consultants over the years. His work these days focuses on helping organizations align business strategies with suppliers and customers, while improving value-based technical processes. His passion is in developing processes to make rapid, high-return improvement in organization performance. He can be reached at mike@wolfgate.org.

Philip Mix works as an independent consultant, based in London (U.K.). His work is primarily in the areas of organizational culture change and team and leadership development. He has helped diverse management teams and workforces in companies and countries in Europe, Africa, Southeast Asia and, most recently, the Middle East. His early work life in the United States included seven years as a community organizer in neighborhoods facing disinvestment, decline, and racial conflict. He can be contacted at philip.mix@totalise.co.uk.

Kenneth Murrell, Ph.D., has been engaged in OD work for over thirty years and started his career working with Gordon Lippitt, Jerry Harvey, and Peter Vaill at George Washington University. Murrell spent a decade working with United Nations projects in Europe and Africa and has traveled to countries around the world doing research on global OD. He is tenured at the University of West Florida, where he helped start the first southern OD program, and is now also core faculty for the Pepperdine doctoral program in organizational change and founding faculty for the Chicago-based Whole-Systems Design master's program of Antioch University. He has also been a guest professor and consultant in Cairo for two years and has been on lecture tours to England, Malta, and Scotland and a frequent guest at the University of Monterrey in Mexico. He can be reached at kmurrell@uwf.edu.

Jean Neumann provides professional advice and development for consultants, managers, and other change agents. In addition to a private practice specializing in organizational change with integrity, Neumann serves The Tavistock Institute as director of studies for its Advanced Organisational Consultation programme. Since 1971, she has undertaken over four hundred consulting and research projects in Europe and the United States. She has a master's degree in adult developmental theory and a doctorate in organizational behavior. Contact her at jean.neumann@btinternet.com.

Phil Nimtz is co-founder of Equinox Training, Inc., and has more than sixteen years of experience in training design, group facilitation, and organization development. He offers interpersonal skills programs, including team development, feedback for performance, leadership, and strategic management. Nimtz is currently pursuing a Ph.D. in human and organization development through the Fielding Graduate Institute.

Chuck Phillips co-founded Reddy * Phillips with his former partner, W. Brendan Reddy. With over thirty years' experience in business and industry in both operating roles—manufacturing, finance, labor relations, human resources management—and internal and external consulting, Phillips brings a unique, integrated perspective to his work.

Day **Piercy,** convenor of CreateNetwork™, has worked in organization development and public policy arenas for over thirty years as a community organizer, entrepreneur, facilitator, consultant, and trainer. Piercy publishes the *CreateNet*® *Connection* newsletter and offers services in meeting facilitation, management, and public policy and training in teamwork, leadership, and collaboration. She can be reached at daypiercy@createnet.com.

Nancy **Polend** is the OD manager at the American Public Human Services Association, whose members are state and local human services agencies. She provides consulting and training to member agencies, primarily in the areas of leadership, high performance, and leading change. Her B.A. is from the Union Institute, and she received a certificate in human resources management from the University of Virginia.

Nancy **Roggen** is senior manager of organizational learning for IMS Health, which provides solutions to issues facing the pharmaceutical industry. She holds an MSOD from AU/NTL.

Jonathan **Ross** consults in performance improvement, implementing change, and leadership development, helping people deal with challenges like working virtually, maintaining alignment with business objectives, and harnessing motivation. Ross has a bachelor's degree from Vassar College and a juris doctor degree from Temple University School of Law. Active in the OD Network and OD Institute, he has facilitated and consulted in a wide variety of forums, from Paris and Dublin to Nebraska and the Mississippi Delta.

Gary **Rossi** is an organizational effectiveness coach, helping organizations achieve business performance excellence through the use of the Malcolm Baldrige Criteria for Performance. He emphasizes strategic planning, performance scorecards and measurement development, process management, and leadership development. Rossi combines his leadership experience gained from leading teams in the Navy's elite SEAL/UDT teams and bomb disposal teams with the skills acquired while coaching sports teams. He holds a master's degree in business and organizational management with an emphasis in total quality management from the University of Redlands. Previously, as a Booz Allen Hamilton consultant, he coached an Internal Revenue Service team through organizational redesign using the Baldrige Criteria. Contact him at garyrossi@csmintl.com.

Cathy Royal, Ph.D., is the founder of IMAGINE US: The Diversity Institute, a not-for-profit dedicated to research, training, and dialogue to promote social and structural justice. Her passion is using Appreciative Inquiry to promote social justice. A trainer for NTL and the NTL Institute Ken Benne Scholar, she has specialties in structural equality and systems thinking, race and gender relations, Appreciative Inquiry, and organizational transformation. Royal designs and conducts training in each of these areas for corporations, foundations, educational institutions, and international agencies and donors. She is the co-editor of *Lessons from the Field: Applying Appreciative Inquiry*.

Patty Sadallah has been an OD consultant/trainer since 1982 and received her master's of organization development from AU/NTL in 1987. Sadallah's consulting practice, Strength in Partners, Inc., in the Cleveland, Ohio, area, helps non-profit and public social service systems partner for greater impact in the community. Her work is about leadership and community development, multi-system development, and the power of strong organizational values to transform a community. She is the co-creator of the Management Success Sequence and Strategic Marketing Model and author of the *Body of Skills for Leading Change*. Reach her at psadallah@strengthinpartners.org.

Jo Sanzgiri is currently a full professor at Alliant International University in the College of Organizational Studies. She has been teaching, conducting research, and consulting in the area of organization development since 1972. Her particular areas of specialization are core values in management, executive coaching, business ethics, and international organization development. She teaches and consults in North America, Latin America, and South Asia. Her research articles have appeared in *Organizational Dynamics*, *The International Journal of Management*, and *The International Journal of Business Ethics*. She is also a published and award-winning poet and writer of fiction. She has recently been named as one of "The Ten Most Influential Women in OD, in the U.S. and Globally" by Benedictine University.

Bev Scott has been a consultant to organizations for over twenty-five years. Her current work includes coaching and development of internal consultants in OD, performance improvement, workplace learning, and human resources. Scott served for fifteen years as director of organization and management development for McKesson Corporation. She is the author of *Consulting on the Inside: An Internal Consultant's Guide to Living and Working Inside Organizations.* She is currently serving as chair of the OD Network board of trustees.

Edith Whitfield Seashore has been consulting to industrial, military, education, and voluntary organizations for the past forty years. Seashore has served as the president of NTL Institute for Applied Behavioral Science and is the recipient of the Organization Development Network Lifetime Achievement Award. In addition to her consulting, she teaches, writes, and serves on advisory boards. She can be reached at 410–997–2828.

Carole Lyles Shaw is founder and president of the Columbia Resource Group; her clients include the World Bank, the Potomac Electric Power Company, the National Association of State Arts Agencies, Goddard Space Flight Center, and other government and commercial clients. Since 1989, she has provided leadership development, executive team retreat facilitation, large group retreat facilitation, and numerous training workshops. Shaw has been invited to speak on leadership, change management, and emotional intelligence at many national and regional conferences. She is a member of the NTL Institute for Applied Behavioral Science and teaches OD in the Georgetown and American University graduate programs. She received an MBA from Columbia University and is pursuing doctoral work at USC. Information about her firm is available at www.ColumbiaRG.com.

Allon Shevat was educated at McGill University and returned to Israel in 1968. Shevat left the Israel Defense Forces as a career officer in the late 1970s and, since 1980, has been a principal and managing director of GR Institute of Organizational Development, headquartered in Tel Aviv. Shevat spends his time in Southeast Asia, Canada, China, America, Japan, and, of course, Tel Aviv, Israel. His fields of interest include managing across international borders, virtual organization, and the management of very aggressive commitments, multi-client OD interventions, and global OD in an acutely diverse environment. Contact him at allons@israel mail.com.

David Sibbet is head of The Grove Consultants International. He is an organizational consultant, information designer, and graphic facilitator, working with clients throughout Europe, North America, and Asia in many different industries. In addition, he has been a research fellow at the Institute for the Future in Menlo Park, California, since 1988. His publications include *Leading Business Teams* (1991) and *Global Work* (1994).

Andrea Sigetich provides management and leadership development consulting and professional leadership coaching. Prior to opening her own business, she had twenty years of internal OD, HR, and leadership development experience. She works from her home in Bend, Oregon.

Jim Smith is a partner in Resources For Change and has been an OD consultant for twenty-five years. He has worked as an external consultant for Shell Canada, as an internal consultant at Bell Northern Research in Ottawa, and as a corporate manager of OD services for 3M Company. His master's in OB is from Brigham Young University.

Peter F. Sorensen, Jr., Ph.D., is professor and director of the Ph.D.-OD program and the MS-MOB program at Benedictine University. With more than two hundred publications, he is past chair of the OD&C Division of the Academy of Management and received the "Outstanding OD Consultant of the Year Award" from the OD Institute.

Helene C. Sugarman is charter co-owner of AIC, LLC, and has been the principal of Dynamic Communication since 1989. She holds an M.A. from Case-Western Reserve University, has a professional certificate in organization development from Georgetown University, and is an adjunct associate professor at University of Maryland-University College (UMUC), where she teaches change management online. Sugarman's clients include government agencies, non-profits, professional associations, boards of directors, high tech companies, medical and healthcare, and educational institutions. Her article, "Appreciative Inquiry (AI): More than a Methodology: Practitioners' Framing for Successful Transformation" was published in *The Channel Marker* (2002).

David **Szymanowski** is involved in changing prisons into a human systems community that will help the inmates become responsible, productive, and law-abiding citizens. He presently is involved in the initial phases of developing his own transitional coaching and mentoring business, LyfeShifts. In his work on transitions, he concentrates on growing experiences and growing potential.

Robert **Tobin** is a consultant, writer, and university lecturer with a focus on doing business in Asia. He is professor of business and commerce at Keio University in Tokyo and visiting professor of commerce and accountancy at Chulalongkorn University in Bangkok. He has worked with more than one hundred organizations in Asia, including Fortune 100 companies and leading Japanese companies. Reach him by email at rtbn@gol.com.

Helene **F. Uhlfelder, Ph.D.,** is the president of WholeSystemAssociates, Inc., a consulting firm that utilizes a holistic approach to complex business problems that integrates strategy, measures, process, technology, and organization factors to assist organizations in achieving bottom-line results. With twenty-five years' experience, including positions with Answerthink, Inc., and Towers Perrin/Miller Howard, Uhlfelder has helped clients achieve business results through strategy development and deployment, organization design, performance measurement and management, leadership development and coaching, and integrated change efforts. She is co-author of three books: *Advanced Team Skills, Whole System Architecture*, and *Change Management.*

Peter **Vaill** is a professor and holder of the distinguished chair in management education in the College of Business, University of St. Thomas, Minneapolis-St. Paul, Minnesota. In his long career as an OD specialist, he has served on the management faculties of UCLA, the University of Connecticut, and The George Washington University, where he was also dean of the School of Business and Public Management for a time. He has authored numerous papers on OD and has authored three books: *Managing as a Performing Art (1989), Learning as a Way of Being* (1996), and *Spirited Leading and Learning* (1998), all published by Jossey-Bass. He has consulted to many corporations, public agencies, health systems, institutions of higher education, and professional associations. He has been a member of the OD Network since its inception and was a founding member of the current form of NTL. In 2002, he was given a Lifetime Achievement Award by the OD Network and was a co-awardee of the David L. Bradford Outstanding Educator Award by the Organizational Behavior Teaching Society.

Valerie **Wallen** serves as the program manager for organization development and accountability for the directorate of the South Carolina Department of Parks, Recreation, and Tourism (PRT). During her private sector experience with the Ohio Manufacturers' Association (OMA), she managed human resource operations and led several statewide programs. She worked with quality programs in several major corporations and led change management efforts in public education, the Ohio legislature, and several companies throughout Ohio. Wallen has an undergraduate degree in education, is an ABA-certified paralegal, and has also served as a senior examiner for the South Carolina Governor's Quality Award program for several years.

Jane **Magruder Watkins** is a past chair of the NTL Institute for Applied Behavioral Science who has worked in the field of organization development for thirty-five years. She has worked in nearly fifty countries on five continents and has been at the forefront of the development of Appreciative Inquiry (AI), an organizational transformation process that enables the kind of agile organization needed to succeed in a constantly changing environment. She is an innovative consultant who pioneered the use of OD and AI in nongovernmental organizations across the globe.

Paul **Wayne** is presently active in Russia, as he has been for the last fourteen years. He is an OD, management development, and performance consultant using strategic HR interventions to help organizations realize their human potential. He says, "In my geocultural area of specialization, the population who need what I do is quite dense. So I have a competitive advantage and I am using it."

Mimi **Weber** has worked primarily in healthcare, with undergraduate degrees in nursing and health administration and a master's degree in human resource development. In her recent involvement in the field of HR administration and employee/labor relations, she enjoys using her OD skills to help organizations create positive work environments that promote productivity and a healthy work/life balance. Reach her at mweber4@bellsouth.net.

Diana Whitney, Ph.D., is an internationally recognized consultant, speaker, and thought leader on the subjects of Appreciative Inquiry, positive change, and spirituality at work. She is an author and editor of numerous books and articles, including *Appreciative Inquiry: An Invitation to a Positive Revolution* and *The Power of Appreciative Inquiry*. Her consulting practice focuses on the use of Appreciative Inquiry for corporate culture change, whole system transformation, merger, alliance and partnership building, and strategic planning. She teaches and consultants in the United States, Europe, and Asia. Whitney's interest in spiritually based postmodern forms of organizing led her to support the design and creation of the United Religions Initiative, a global interfaith organization dedicated to peace and cooperation among people of differing religions, faiths, and spiritual and indigenous traditions. She can be reached at Diana@positivechange.org.

Christopher Worley, Ph.D., is director of the master of science in organization development (MSOD) program and an associate professor of business strategy at Pepperdine University's Graziodio School of Business and Management. He was awarded the Luckman Distinguished Teaching Fellowship in 1997. Prior to his work at Pepperdine University, Worley taught undergraduate and graduate courses at the University of San Diego, University of Southern California, and Colorado State University. He is also president of Monique Marketing and Management, a consulting firm specializing in strategic management. His consulting activities are complemented by more than fifteen years of management experience in academic, for-profit, and government organizations. His many publications include *Integrated Strategic Change: How OD Builds Competitive Advantage* and co-authorship of the fifth, sixth, and seventh editions of *Organization Development and Change*.

Therese Yaeger, Ph.D., is associate director of the OD doctoral program at Benedictine University, where she also teaches OD-OB courses. Her recent publications include *Global and International Organization Development* (with Sorensen, Head, and Cooperrider) and *Appreciative Inquiry: An Emerging Direction for OD* (with Cooperrider, Sorensen, and Whitney).

Index

Pfeiffer Publications Guide

This guide is designed to familiarize you with the various types of Pfeiffer publications. The formats section describes the various types of products that we publish; the methodologies section describes the many different ways that content might be provided within a product. We also provide a list of the topic areas in which we publish.

FORMATS

In addition to its extensive book-publishing program, Pfeiffer offers content in an array of formats, from fieldbooks for the practitioner to complete, ready-to-use training packages that support group learning.

FIELDBOOK Designed to provide information and guidance to practitioners in the midst of action. Most fieldbooks are companions to another, sometimes earlier, work, from which its ideas are derived; the fieldbook makes practical what was theoretical in the original text. Fieldbooks can certainly be read from cover to cover. More likely, though, you'll find yourself bouncing around following a particular theme, or dipping in as the mood, and the situation, dictate.

HANDBOOK A contributed volume of work on a single topic, comprising an eclectic mix of ideas, case studies, and best practices sourced by practitioners and experts in the field.

An editor or team of editors usually is appointed to seek out contributors and to evaluate content for relevance to the topic. Think of a handbook not as a ready-to-eat meal, but as a cookbook of ingredients that enables you to create the most fitting experience for the occasion.

RESOURCE Materials designed to support group learning. They come in many forms: a complete, ready-to-use exercise (such as a game); a comprehensive resource on one topic (such as conflict management) containing a variety of methods and approaches; or a collection of like-minded activities (such as icebreakers) on multiple subjects and situations.

TRAINING PACKAGE An entire, ready-to-use learning program that focuses on a particular topic or skill. All packages comprise a guide for the facilitator/trainer and a workbook for the participants. Some packages are supported with additional media—such as video—or learning aids, instruments, or other devices to help participants understand concepts or practice and develop skills.

- *Facilitator/trainer's guide* Contains an introduction to the program, advice on how to organize and facilitate the learning event, and step-by-step instructor notes. The guide also contains copies of presentation materials—handouts, presentations, and overhead designs, for example—used in the program.

- *Participant's workbook* Contains exercises and reading materials that support the learning goal and serves as a valuable reference and support guide for participants in the weeks and months that follow the learning event. Typically, each participant will require his or her own workbook.

ELECTRONIC CD-ROMs and web-based products transform static Pfeiffer content into dynamic, interactive experiences. Designed to take advantage of the searchability, automation, and ease-of-use that technology provides, our e-products bring convenience and immediate accessibility to your workspace.

METHODOLOGIES

CASE STUDY A presentation, in narrative form, of an actual event that has occurred inside an organization. Case studies are not prescriptive, nor are they used to prove a point; they are designed to develop critical analysis and decision-making skills. A case study has a specific time frame, specifies a sequence of events, is narrative in structure, and contains a plot structure—an issue (what should be/have been done?). Use case studies when the goal is to enable participants to apply previously learned theories to the circumstances in the case, decide what is pertinent, identify the real issues, decide what should have been done, and develop a plan of action.

ENERGIZER A short activity that develops readiness for the next session or learning event. Energizers are most commonly used after a break or lunch to stimulate or refocus the group. Many involve some form of physical activity, so they are a useful way to counter post-lunch lethargy. Other uses include transitioning from one topic to another, where "mental" distancing is important.

EXPERIENTIAL LEARNING ACTIVITY (ELA) A facilitator-led intervention that moves participants through the learning cycle from experience to application (also known as a Structured Experience). ELAs are carefully thought-out designs in which there is a definite learning purpose and intended outcome. Each step—everything that participants do during the activity—facilitates the accomplishment of the stated goal. Each ELA includes complete instructions for facilitating the intervention and a clear statement of goals, suggested group size and timing, materials required, an explanation of the process, and, where appropriate, possible variations to the activity. (For more detail on Experiential Learning Activities, see the Introduction to the *Reference Guide to Handbooks and Annuals*, 1999 edition, Pfeiffer, San Francisco.)

GAME A group activity that has the purpose of fostering team spirit and togetherness in addition to the achievement of a pre-stated goal. Usually contrived—undertaking a desert expedition, for example—this type of learning method offers an engaging means for participants to demonstrate and practice business and interpersonal skills. Games are effective for team building and personal development mainly because the goal is subordinate to the process—the means through which participants reach decisions, collaborate, communicate, and generate trust and understanding. Games often engage teams in "friendly" competition.

ICEBREAKER A (usually) short activity designed to help participants overcome initial anxiety in a training session and/or to acquaint the participants with one another. An icebreaker can be a fun activity or can be tied to specific topics or training goals. While a useful tool in itself, the icebreaker comes into its own in situations where tension or resistance exists within a group.

INSTRUMENT A device used to assess, appraise, evaluate, describe, classify, and summarize various aspects of human behavior. The term used to describe an instrument depends primarily on its format and purpose. These terms include survey, questionnaire, inventory, diagnostic, survey, and poll. Some uses of instruments include providing instrumental feedback to group members, studying here-and-now processes or functioning within a group, manipulating group composition, and evaluating outcomes of training and other interventions.

Instruments are popular in the training and HR field because, in general, more growth can occur if an individual is provided with a method for focusing specifically on his or her own behavior. Instruments also are used to obtain information that will serve as a basis for change and to assist in workforce planning efforts.

Paper-and-pencil tests still dominate the instrument landscape with a typical package comprising a facilitator's guide, which offers advice on administering the instrument and interpreting the collected data, and an initial set of instruments. Additional instruments are available separately. Pfeiffer, though, is investing heavily in e-instruments. Electronic instrumentation provides effortless distribution and, for larger groups particularly, offers advantages over paper-and-pencil tests in the time it takes to analyze data and provide feedback.

LECTURETTE A short talk that provides an explanation of a principle, model, or process that is pertinent to the participants' current learning needs. A lecturette is intended to establish a common language bond between the trainer and the participants by providing a mutual frame of reference. Use a lecturette as an introduction to a group activity or event, as an interjection during an event, or as a handout.

MODEL A graphic depiction of a system or process and the relationship among its elements. Models provide a frame of reference and something more tangible, and more easily remembered, than a verbal explanation. They also give participants something to "go on," enabling them to track their own progress as they experience the dynamics, processes, and relationships being depicted in the model.

ROLE PLAY A technique in which people assume a role in a situation/scenario: a customer service rep in an angry-customer exchange, for example. The way in which the role is approached is then discussed and feedback is offered. The role play is often repeated using a different approach and/or incorporating changes made based on feedback received. In other words, role playing is a spontaneous interaction involving realistic behavior under artificial (and safe) conditions.

SIMULATION A methodology for understanding the interrelationships among components of a system or process. Simulations differ from games in that they test or use a model that depicts or mirrors some aspect of reality in form, if not necessarily in content. Learning occurs by studying the effects of change on one or more factors of the model. Simulations are commonly used to test hypotheses about what happens in a system—often referred to as "what if?" analysis—or to examine best-case/worst-case scenarios.

THEORY A presentation of an idea from a conjectural perspective. Theories are useful because they encourage us to examine behavior and phenomena through a different lens.

TOPICS

The twin goals of providing effective and practical solutions for workforce training and organization development and meeting the educational needs of training and human resource professionals shape Pfeiffer's publishing program. Core topics include the following:

Leadership & Management

Communication & Presentation

Coaching & Mentoring

Training & Development

e-Learning

Teams & Collaboration

OD & Strategic Planning

Human Resources

Consulting